M000208587

Who Cares What You Think?
It's All BS Anyway!

Thoughts on the Origins
of Personal Stories

James Sibley

Fulton Books, Inc.
Meadville, PA

Published by Fulton Books 2020

ISBN 978-1-64654-596-4 (paperback)
ISBN 978-1-64654-597-1 (digital)

Printed in the United States of America

Contents

Acknowledgements

Support can be defined as giving assistance or enabling action to complete a given task. The perception of support is, as most things are, a story that emanates from the experience of completing the task. The following people were, knowingly or unknowingly, meaningful contributors to the completion of this effort by providing needed inspiration and support during times of challenge.

I owe a debt of gratitude to my wife Diane for her love and persistent encouragement; my children Shanda and Jamaal for being an ongoing source of pride and inspiration; my 'moms' and 'pops' (Mary and Justice) for their lifelong love, patience and motivation; my brother Jerome for his unwavering support and belief in my abilities; and my friends Jerry Scott and Ron Dukes for their friendly challenge and early help crystallizing the idea for the book. I would also like thank Jay Morris, John and Terri Pedace, Rhona and Rick Reagen, Judith Kaplan-Weinger and Julie Benesh for reigniting interest and providing needed energy and support at critical times in the process.

I want to add a special note of love and appreciation for my "pops," Justice Raymond Mallard, who passed away July 11, 2020.

Finally, I want to thank God for his goodness, grace and mercy—through, by and with whom all things are possible (as evidenced by the completion of this, my first writing endeavor).

I. BS

Stories that we hear or make up can be
descriptive, reflective, entertaining, informative or reassuring. They can be used to
describe or explain every human experi-
ence or condition. Our process of creating
stories is heavily influenced by our inclinations toward a certain way of thinking
or view of the world. These inclinations
reveal themselves in the form of biases.

I recently had a dialogue, debate, heated discussion—well, really,
an argument with a friend about who was the greatest basketball
player of all time. If any of you have been misguided enough to ever
engage in such an exchange, you know this topic can heat up faster
than a blister bug in a pepper patch (Southern for getting very hot
very fast).

Our discussion began with a very cordial exchange of opinions. My choice for the best player of all time was none other than
the incomparable king of the sky and immortalized Nike fly-guy,
Michael Jordan. His was LeBron James.

Please allow me to digress for a moment. Did you notice how I
introduced each player? I've already labeled Michael "the incomparable king of the sky" and "immortalized Nike fly-guy." This just points
out how I (not so subtly) began "selling" my belief even before sharing any real evidence. I even avoided using LeBron's commonly used
moniker "King" James, which would have implicitly elevated him to
the status of basketball royalty without further attribution. After all,
there can only be one person deserving of the title "king of basketball," and we all know that's none other than Michael Jordan. So I've
already made my true beliefs "figural," or the main focus of what I'm
sharing. It follows that most of the evidence that I choose will strongly
support my BS and, taking it one step further, discredit the BS of anyone with an opposing point of view. Such is the evolution of today's

political discourse; vote for my BS, which is the "truth," rather than the other guys" BS, which is obviously "untrue" *even before examining any facts*. But I'm sure none of you have ever personally done this. Well, maybe some. Well, probably quite a few. Well, most likely all have done this at one time or another. Just take a moment to think about it. Now back to the discussion I had with my friend.

Not to berate anyone's basketball IQ, but is there anyone who doesn't know Michael Jordan or Lebron James? Here's just a little background for the .0001% of the world's population who hasn't heard of either.

Michael Jordan played most of his career with the Chicago Bulls (1984–1999, with a brief midcareer retirement in 1993). He was a member of six NBA championship teams, fourth all-time in field goals made, fourth all-time in free throws made, second all-time in steals, third all-time in points, first all-time in points per game, third all-time in steals per game, fourteen-time NBA All-Star, Rookie of the Year, Defensive Player of the Year, five-time NBA MVP, six-time NBA Finals MVP, eleven-time All-NBA selection, and nine-time All-Defensive Team selection.

LeBron James was drafted directly out of high school and was the first overall pick of the 2003 NBA Draft by the Cleveland Cavaliers. He was a member of three NBA championship teams, received four NBA MVP Awards, three NBA Finals MVP Awards, and two Olympic Gold Medals. Fifteen-time NBA All-Star and three NBA All-Star MVP Awards, all-time NBA playoff scoring leader, forth in all-time career points, ninth in all-time assists, and all NBA Defensive First Team five times.

I informed my obviously confused friend that Michael Jordan was the greatest of all time because he was mentally and physically the greatest athlete ever to play the game. He was an exceptional player on both offense and defense. His greatness is almost unquestioned, and he is revered like no other. His name is synonymous with basketball, not only in the US, but throughout the world. No one else even comes close. He is undoubtedly the greatest of all times.

But my friend countered with an equally compelling picture of LeBron. He insisted that Lebron was the most versatile player in the history of the game; an incomparable prototype of big point guard and one of the best passing small forwards ever to play the game. He went on to say that LeBron's size, versatility, and agility made him almost impossible to stop. No one made the game look easier. His court sense was unparalleled, and his ability to seamlessly move from small forward to point guard made him more versatile than anyone in the history of the game.

Both players obviously had very impressive résumés and a significant amount of data to support either being considered the "best." We were both easily able to justify our belief in the rightness of our perspectives.

This begs the question "Who was right?" Of course, the obvious answer is me. I'm always right—in my mind. But how do we seriously approach answering this question? Easy enough, you might say. Why not just look at the data and agree that the player with the best stats is the best player? Right? Wrong! You would think that if we just stuck to the facts—compare apples to apples—the answer to our quest to find the best would become glaringly obvious. I'm sure this assumption has been a source of much frustration for many of those who consider themselves objective, impartial, and unbiased thinkers.

(It reminds me of the line from *Dragnet*, a radio and television crime drama about the cases handled by a dedicated Los Angeles police detective by the name of Sergeant Joe Friday. One of Sergeant Friday's favorite lines has become one of the most iconic lines in TV history—"Just the facts, ma'am." Joe Friday's deadpan, straight-faced delivery of that line was never a surprise, but always entertaining. I used to love that show.)

Back to the question at hand, how do we determine "the best"? To identify the best, the options being considered, in this case Michael Jordan and LeBron James, should be measured against a set of clearly defined standards. These standards are often referred to as "selection criteria." This is where BS rears its ugly head. What selection criteria do we use? Should the criteria be quantitative—the most NBA championships, the most MVP awards, the most All-Star appearances, the most points, the most assists, the most rebounds...? Or should the criteria be qualitative—the player that performed the best in the most important performance categories, the player that did the best job of facilitating teamwork, the player that was most popular among fans...? Or should it be a combination of both? I would venture to guess that most would choose option three—"a combination of both." Problem solved, right? I think not. This is actually just the tip of the iceberg—the beginning of the process of selecting, reconciling differences, and ultimately, agreeing on a decision that is mutually beneficial and satisfying.

There are a couple of reasons that this process is so difficult. First, *we selectively choose facts that either support our beliefs or serve our interests.* And secondly, *we find ways to either rationalize, dispel, or ignore any facts that don't.*

Many will claim and probably believe that their decisions and choices are completely unbiased, based purely on facts. And I agree that relatable facts can be found to support just about any choice. However, given the same set of facts, each person can hear, interpret, and respond to them differently. The facts that we choose, the meanings that we infer, and the resulting actions that we take are more reflective of our biases than our objectivity.

Our willingness to reconcile differences depends on the level of importance we place on the issue being discussed. I think I can safely assume that agreeing on who's the best basketball player of all time is probably not high on anyone's priority list. In most of our lives, we have much larger fish to fry. But any difference of opinion can hold the embers of potential discord.

I recently read an interesting article about the seeds of potential discord involving an issue in the United Methodist Church that had been simmering for some time and was now on the verge of exploding (Methodist Church has reached its breaking point by Guthrie Graves-Fitzsimmons). The United Methodist Church represents the largest denomination of the Protestant religion. In existence since the eighteenth century, the church recently announced plans to split into two autonomous wings; the "traditionalist" wing and the "liberal reform" wing. The reported reason for the split was that the liberal wing supported gay marriage and LGBTQ clergy, which the traditionalist wing was adamantly opposed to. This led to a protracted and highly contentious relationship between the two wings for decades. Once again, "who's right?" and "what criteria should be used to determine who's right?"

Generally, self-righteousness can lead to intolerance. The aforementioned traditionalist wing of United Methodist Church initially proposed that sanctions be imposed on clergy that violated their "tradition" of exclusion. These sanctions included suspensions, fines, and potential expulsion for pastors who performed gay marriages. Conversely, the more liberal wing wanted to ensure that the rights and dignity of the LGBTQ community were respected.

It's amazing how often we make the perceived "rightness" of our perspective the same as the "truth" of our perspective. My personal story is that there is only one Truth, with a capital "T," and many shades of truth, with a small "t," and it can be extremely difficult to discern the difference between the two. This book is for those of us who live in the world of small *t*'s, leaving the capital *T*s to those who are much more enlightened than I could ever hope to be (i.e., the philosophers, the prophets, the scientists).

Most of us have heard and perhaps even used the acronym BS at some point in our lives. It is commonly used as an abbreviation for the expletive "bulls—t." This use of *BS* usually has a negative connotation and refers to something that is considered blatantly untrue. But as we all know, that "something" that one person views as blatantly untrue can be viewed by another as indisputably valid. So rather than using BS in this very limited context, I've expanded its meaning to include all perspectives, be they true, false, or indifferent.

Let's get something clear right away. BS doesn't mean what you might think it means. It's not the expletive we commonly use to describe disingenuous, misleading, or false information. It's not the phrase that is often hurled in a deprecating way at something we are unwilling or unable to accept as true. It's not the equivalent of animal excretion. If you have any knowledge of English slang at all, I'm almost certain that *BS* is not foreign to your language acumen (that means you know what it is).

I've come not to destroy the phrase but, rather, to expand its meaning and significance. You might be thinking "expand its meaning and significance, why? I know all I need to know about BS. As a matter of fact, I would even consider myself an expert on BS." Hold on just a minute. This is not intended to denigrate your expertise in BS. This is being written during the season of a highly contested presidential race, and I have ample evidence that there is a lot of BS expertise out there.

Let me begin by sharing a strongly held personal belief—we all have a lot of BS in us. Some might even venture to say "we're full of BS." But before you ban me from your next Bible study group or put me on your list of undesirables, please let me explain. What I mean is that we all have some of what I choose to call the *new BS*, in addition to a lot of the old BS we all know and love. And what, you might ask, is "the new BS?" Pay attention because BS will underpin everything that follows and will be referenced repeatedly. You've already been introduced to BS in the book's title. Are you ready for this? The new BS is *biased stories!*

I think most of us would agree that we see things through different lenses. These lenses are an amalgamation of what we've learned from a lifetime of experiences. They reflect our personal biases and vary from person to person. Often, we can see the exact same thing and see it quite differently, leading to completely different perspectives about that experience's meaning, significance, and impact. These differing stories can lead us down the path of distortion, confusion, and conflict or, antithetically, the path of inquiry, insight, and innovation.

All stories are multidimensional. They have discrete (separate and distinct) origins and serve a wide variety of purposes, either to express a thought, solve a problem, or inform an action. Stories are a core tool of communication. They enhance our ability to comprehend and engage in meaningful dialogue. Every thought we have, question we ask, or statement we make is either the product of or antecedent to a story. Stories are constantly shifting and changing with every new experience. From these experiences, we construct and share stories that bring others, at times kicking and screaming, into our consciousness.

When I worked eons ago in information technology (IT), there was a simple model we used to develop information processing programs. The acronym was IPO, which stood for input-process-output. There was also a companion phrase to IPO called GIGO or garbage in, garbage out. In combination, IPO and GIGO essentially implied that there was a direct correlation between the quality of a program's input and the accuracy of its output; if bad in, then bad out, and conversely, if good in, then good out. The purpose of this simple structure was to ensure that quality input was run through a quality process to produce consistently reliable quality results.

Interestingly enough, a similar IPO structure can be used to create stories. When creating stories, we selectively take things in (input), we process what we take in through our internal filters (process), and then draw some sort of conclusion about what it all means (output). However, unlike IT, the inputs for stories are random, the processes variable, and the outputs unpredictable. In the IT world, that probably wouldn't be a good thing. However, in the world of stories, unpredictability is the norm rather than the exception. It is the underlying force that drives creative thought.

There is a scripture in the Bible that says, "For whatever a man soweth, that shall he also reap." This generally has a negative connotation that implies that one suffers consequences that are commensurate with their actions; bad actions will lead to bad consequences, and conversely, good actions will drive good consequences. Like IPO, it implies that there is a direct correlation between what goes in and what comes out. Individuals quite naturally take different things in, see things differently, and more often than not, come to different conclusions. These conclusions are reflected in the stories we create. These stories influence every life choice we make from the clothes we wear to the food we eat to the relationships we build to the faiths we believe.

Expanding the biblical metaphor, developing a story is like planting a seed, nurturing its growth, and reaping its harvest. Planting the seeds is like the input phase of story creation. It is the initial conscious or subconscious process of forming an idea—something I call *inspiration*. Nurturing a story's growth is what I call *assimilation*, or the process of giving an idea concrete form, structure, and meaning. The harvesting of a story's fruits I call *integration*, or the process of blending newly formed ideas with other thoughts to form a congruent "whole"—*inspiration, assimilation,* and *integration* (or if you prefer—plant, nurture, and harvest).

It's difficult to understand what stimulates the creation of any given story. We construct stories naturally, either intentionally (through purposeful actions of our conscious mind), experientially (through experience-related observations and reflections), or subliminally (through signals "audible" only to our unconscious mind). The facts we choose, the meaning we attribute to those facts, and the corresponding stories we create are unique to the person. Stories can grow from a sensation, an observation, an inspiration, or any number of conscious or subconscious forms of stimulation. Some stories originate from and are supported by rigorous investigative research. Some stories are the product of a random thought or fleeting observation. And still others are impressions that you didn't know existed that reside in the recesses of your subconscious mind. All experiences are potential fodder for creative thought. We selectively choose facts from each experience that captures our interest. With this dynamic interplay between our conscious and unconscious minds, it is virtually impossible to determine any story's true origin, path of creation, or clear destination. The more conscious effort required to create a story, the greater the understanding of the story's roots, where the story started, and how and why it was created.

The stories we create are ever present, though not always readily obvious to us. "How can that be?" you might ask. "I create stories that I don't even know I've created?" Well, yes. The conscious and subconscious minds are always at work and play key roles in story creation. Case in point is a study conducted by Marianne Bertrand of the University of Chicago and Sendhil Mullainathan of Harvard that found differences in the treatment of African Americans and whites in immigration, employment, housing, and the criminal justice system. Some might immediately respond, "Tell me something I don't know." But wait, there was something I found to be interesting in the study's findings. A question arose as to whether the noted differences were pure acts of discrimination or not.

The study concluded that economists tended to group explanations of discriminatory behavior into two buckets: *taste-based* and *statistical*. By way of example, if a service industry employee (librarian) chose not to respond to a client's inquiry because they knew that person was black, that would be considered taste-based discrimination or, more bluntly, blatant racism. "Statistical" discrimination, on the other hand, occurs when a service person sees a person's name and uses it as a personal marker for other characteristics. Perhaps an African American–sounding name signals that a person is more likely to be poor. The person happens to be biased against poor people. In this case, race is being used as a statistic for inferring poverty, and it's the perception of poverty that causes the discriminatory behavior. Taste-based discrimination, or racism, isn't necessarily the result of conscious thought. One of the study's authors said that it's possible "this behavior is due to some sort of unconscious bias" and "making people aware of the problem may contribute to the solution."

If awareness really is the first step toward a solution, then the study may be helpful in refining our understanding of racial discrimination in America. It occurs (linkages) not only in the labor market and the criminal justice system, but also in countless small interactions every day. The culprit may not be a hate-spewing white nationalist but, rather, a librarian, school administrator, or a county clerk, unaware that he or she is helping some clients more than others.

New stories seamlessly emanate from and reflect our values and beliefs. They are therefore inherently biased. Awareness of these biases can have profound implications in how we view and engage with others and the world we live in. They can be the difference between success and failure, love and hate, war and peace, and indeed, life and death. This may sound somewhat hyperbolic, but I invite you to look at the amount of chaos in the world today having its origins in biased thinking (e.g., racial tension, social upheaval, political conflict, religious dissent).

The purpose of this book is not to make you an expert at creating stories. According to most social psychologists, we're all pretty adept at doing that already. Instead, it will hopefully lead you to see the process of constructing and deconstructing stories as a practical tool for creating *greater awarenesses* of your stories, leading to *greater sensitivity* to the stories of others, resulting in a *greater understanding* of how our individual and collective stories affect the world around us.

Here are some of the questions I attempt to address:

- Why do we believe what we believe?
- Why is it that once we believe something, it's so hard to change (no matter how much evidence to the contrary)?
- What are biases and how do they affect the choices that we make and the actions that we take?
- Why do we believe some people more than we believe others?

Other related topics include the following:

- Who we uniquely are
- How that affects what we pay attention to and believe
- How we receive, process, and share information
- How all these things influence our worldview and ability to adapt and change

Getting Real about BS

Let me begin with a personal confession. Sad but true, I believed in Santa Claus and the tooth fairy well into my preadolescent years—partially because it was advantageous for me to do so with the gifts and all. But mostly because I just wanted to believe that the positive spirit and energy of such beings had to have some basis in reality.

Now that I'm well into middle age (some might even say that I'm old), I still, at times, like to indulge in the fantasies of my youth. Perhaps not in the same way, but I still want to believe that there were some real beings that actually walked the earth that were the beginnings of such well-preserved and widely shared myths as Santa and the tooth fairy.

How did the stories of Santa Claus and the tooth fairy originate? I'm sure there must have been a real person who lived long ago that was middle aged, prematurely gray, stout, jovial, and adored children so much that if they were of good parental report, he gave them gifts during the Christmas season. Likewise, I'm sure there was another person—who knows, perhaps even a dentist of olden time— who promised children a wonderful reward from a secret source if they would just be patient and calm during a challenging dental procedure. Only afterward instructing the parents to secretly slip a treat under their pillow as they slept while recovering from the ordeal. (Just an aside, I read somewhere that some children received upward of twenty dollars per tooth. I think I received a quarter. So according to my calculation, given time and compound interest, my parents owe me $553.22.)

For me, Santa and the tooth fairy were as real as rain, as solid as an oak tree, and as reliable as the sun. However, no matter how solid and reliable the myth might be, there are always some doubting Thomases around to mess things up. My best friend happened to be one of those.

I didn't realize how perceptually challenged he was until one day when we were both about eight years old and he boldly proclaimed, "You know, my parents have been trying to make me believe that Santa Claus puts those gifts under the Christmas tree. I play along. But I know there is no Santa Claus!"

No Santa Claus! How mentally defective was he? At that time, I didn't have the guts to tell him how misguided and ill-informed he was. But secretly, I decided it was time for me to find a more intelligent best friend—which thankfully, I never shared with him, because to this day I would never have been able to live it down.

There are several things that are noteworthy about my little trip down fantasy lane. First, I was strongly influenced by the information that I received from trusted sources—that being my parents (so, parents, be careful what you tell your kids).

Secondly, my experience, as limited and uninformed as it might have been, became the dominant lens through which I determined "the truth" (I say go with what you "know"). I developed a strong attachment to what many would consider an unsubstantiated belief at such an early age (and those "many" would of course be wrong—at least about the unsubstantiated part).

And thirdly, once my truth was established, it was difficult for me to acknowledge that there might be another "truth" out there as valid as mine (certainly not possible). How easily I judged my friend's trustworthiness based on what I perceived to be his lack of acceptance or willingness to acknowledge what was unquestionably, undeniably, unmistakably, indelibly, definitively, absolutely the "truth."

Some might say that I had no real data that could possibly support the existence of either Santa Claus or the tooth fairy. But I would beg to differ. I had data from the most dependable and reliable source any young preadolescent child could have—my parents. Their word was golden. It needed no cosigner or any other form of substantiation. It simply stood on its own. If anyone had data to the contrary, well they could just take that data and, mildly put, shove it in a bottle and toss it in the ocean. (What did you think I was going to say?)

So *we selectively choose data based on its perceived credibility*. The data's credibility is more often than not determined by how consistent it is with what we already believe. In this case, my belief was not necessarily based on the data that was shared, but in who shared the data.

Had I not given you such a detailed account of the origins, or you had not otherwise been informed, my story would've worked just as well as the real ones. You know I'm right. No matter which versions of the story you choose to believe, it's still just that—a story. *Stories are the imaginative creations of the right side of our brain peppered with a few facts to add spice.* They are often based on past events that we felt were important enough to add to our memory bank for future reference.

Sustainable stories are generally time tested for quality and reliability (sounds a lot like an auto sales commercial, doesn't it?). An

important thing to remember is that stories, whether real or fictitious, can live in infamy if they meet the test of meaning, purpose,
and reliability.

If you think about these stories, they generally

- had simple beginnings,
- evolved over time,
- served a specific purpose,
- had personal meaning, and
- were believed to be consistently reliable theories of "truth."

"Okay," you might say, so perhaps I was a little gullible when
I was young. But now that I'm a full-grown adult, I've turned away
from childish things. I'm no longer susceptible to the whimsical fantasies of my youth. I would never ever fall for stories today that were
so obviously untrue. I can now easily discern that which is true from
that which is contrived. Or can I? What do you think about the following often repeated stories?

- There's a natural chemical in turkey that makes you sleepy
  after a Thanksgiving meal.
  (It's not the turkey but the cheap wine, bad conversation
  and carb-filled meal that makes you sleepy.)
- When having a conversation with a person from Japan, it's
  rude to make direct eye contact.
  (Maybe this was true during the reign of emperor Taisho,
  but not today.)
- "Irregardless" is a word.
  (Not! Since "ir" means "not" as in irregular and irresponsi-
  ble, what does not-regardless mean?)
- Bulls are only enraged and charge when they see the color
  red.
  (Try walking inconspicuously across an open field where
  a bull is grazing wearing all white and see what happens.
  Good luck!)

- Bananas grow on trees.
  (Everybody has seen a "banana tree." Yes, but no. The banana trees you may have seen were in fact "herbaceous flowering plants" with a trunk made of rolled leaves. Who woulda thought?)
- Humans and dinosaurs coexisted on earth.
  (Only in the movies. The last of the dinosaurs died 65.5 million years ago, and the earliest human form appeared between 2.3 and 2.4 million years ago.)
- Sugar causes hyperactivity in children.
  (Clinical trials have shown no difference in behavior between children given high sugar and sugar-free diets. Yahoo! Bring on the Ben and Jerry's Cherry Garcia.)
- People only use ten percent of their brains.
  (By choice, not by physiological design. This myth is believed to have started with psychologist and philosopher William James, who supposedly once used the "ten percent" expression metaphorically.)
- Lightning never strikes the same place twice.
  (If you believe this one, try standing at the highest point of the Empire State Building during a lightning storm.)
- Shaving causes hair to grow back thicker, coarser and darker.
  (I've been shaving my understated mustache and beard for years, hoping this one was true.)
- Reading in the dark will ruin your eyes.
  (My son use to read in the dark and he's blind as a bat today. Oh, by the way, bats aren't blind.)
- If you swallow gum, it takes at least a year for it to pass through your digestive system.
  (This makes all the sense in the world with gum being so sticky and all.)

These are beliefs that others might find relatively innocuous and, perhaps, even amusing. You're probably thinking, "Nope, not me. I never believed any of these things." But I'm sure if you think hard enough, you'll realize that at some point in your life, you were bamboozled with some truism from your parents, the church, a friend, an "expert," or a politician that you swallowed whole without question. It might be possible that I'm the only one, but I don't think so. Let's try some beliefs that are more volatile in the domain of public opinion.

- Global warming is a myth.
- Capital punishment is inhumane.
- Gay marriage is sacrilegious.
- Abortion is immoral.
- Minorities are oppressed in the U.S.
- Any laws restricting gun ownership violate the Second Amendment rights.
- Using marijuana can result in long-term cognitive impairment.
- Freedom of speech is an inherent individual right.
- God created heaven and earth, and Jesus is the Son of God.

Of course, the second grouping of topics are much more complex and multidimensional than the first. Some might consider these topics too controversial. But for me, there is no too controversial. Though there is an incredible amount of data on these topics, our intuition allows us to quickly form an opinion without a lot of detailed reasoning. These topics can invoke a different level of emotional response depending on your knowledge of, belief in, and attachment to each. But the way your opinion about each topic initially formed and ultimately evolved (knowledge), the level of acceptance and credibility (belief), and the intensity of personal value and meaning (attachment) follow the same developmental path as your early childhood stories.

The purpose of this writing is not to discuss ways to either foster agreement, build consensus, or differentiate right from wrong. The purpose is to share thoughts on how one might look at their own stories through "different" eyes to help create new awarenesses about ourselves by examining our stories, their origins, and their purpose for being. And taking it one step further, to help us see that *it's all BS anyway*.

It's very difficult for us to remain completely unbiased and indifferent when listening to arguments on either side of any topic. For each there is "the truth" (usually the position we take) and a host of other perspectives—or "personal truths"—that are at best reasonable and, at worst, completely false. Though I may feel that other positions are possible, I believe that any position I take is unquestionably right. Why would I take a position I thought was wrong? (Duh!) They're either right or wrong, black or white, period! What's this shades-of-gray BS? Shades of gray is where most of our BS lives. It is the area that is much less certain and much more divisive.

Personal truths are nothing more than those strongly held uncompromising beliefs that may or may not be true. *The gap between "the truth" and our "personal truths" is where BS lives.* Though we might not want to believe it, for each of our beliefs about any given topic, there can (and quite often is) a significant deviation from the definitive truth. If you think about it, most of us believe that we speak in "truisms." Why would we consciously choose a position that was untrue except to consciously deceive? Just so you know, any future references to *"personal truths"* will only include those *sincerely held beliefs* and not those created to win an argument or gain some sort of personal advantage.

You might say, "Yeah, I may believe some of these stories—but so what! Are you trying to tell me that the stories that I've trusted and believed in for all these years are just figments of my imagination? Are you saying that all, most, some of my stories are not true? I'm going to let you be the judge of that. For me, it's less about the factual accuracy of your story than it is your ability to differentiate between the parts that are fact versus that which is pure conjecture. We often share stories that we agree with or believe to be true despite their inaccuracies. So if it agrees with our sensibilities—if it fits within the boundaries of our beliefs—if it passes our personal credibility test, we give ourselves permission to offer it up as the truth.

This is not a new phenomenon. A case in point, in the Middle Ages, there was a pervasive cosmological view that the earth was flat. Our history books tell us that this belief was one of the obstacles Columbus had to overcome to get his voyage to the new world sanctioned.

Biased stories (BS) are personal thoughts, feelings, and beliefs that creatively combine the facts of our experiences with the fictions of our beliefs to form our personal "truths." Most of us are so skilled at creating these alternative truths that we don't even realize when we've done it. It's second nature. And the world readily supports us in building a repository of BS that guides the way we think, the decisions that we make, and the actions that we take.

If we believe our BS is good for us, why wouldn't we share it with rest of the world? It's always worked for me in the past. And besides that, it worked for my parents, their parents, and even my great-great-great-great-grandparents. So if it worked for all of us, I don't know why it wouldn't work for you.

We not only have to deal with our own BS, we have to deal with the BS of others. We've got family, friend, church, and work BS. We've got local, regional, and cross-continental BS. We've got racial, ethnic, and gender BS. We've got political, social, and economic BS. We have complex, compound, and competing BS, and the list goes on and on. BS is everywhere!

However, even with so much BS in the world, BS in and of itself is not "bad." It just "is." It's how we see and use BS that causes it to be either "good" or "bad." If we see our BS as a self-serving tool for manipulation and distortion, that might be considered bad. If we see it as a possible resource for service and enrichment—helping something or someone to be better—that could be a good thing.

Section 1: BS

Underlying themes

- Why do we believe what we believe?
- Why is it that once we believe something it's so hard to change?

- What are biases and how do they affect our personal choices and actions?
- Why do we believe some people more than we believe others?

Other related topics

- Who we uniquely are.
- How that affects what we pay attention to and believe.
- How we receive, process and share information.
- How all of these things influence our world view and ability to adapt and change.

Stories

- Usually have simple beginnings.
- Evolve (change) over time.
- Serve a specific purpose and have personal meaning (to the creator).
- Are believed to be consistently reliable theories of "truth".
- Can create new insights (awareness) into who we are and what we believe.

Biased Stories

- Creatively combine the facts of our experiences with the fictions of our beliefs to form a "personal truth."
- Live in the gap between "the truth" and our "personal truths."

II. It's Complicated

Explaining how and why stories are created is difficult. Yet creating stories is as natural as breathing; everyone does it whether they know it or not. We are naturally endowed with the ability to form opinions effortlessly about the things we experience.

"In the real world, atoms and molecules are almost never left to themselves; they are almost always exposed to a certain amount of energy and material flowing in from the outside". In life, human systems, like all other natural systems, never evolve in isolation. They are constantly exposed to and acted upon by outside forces. Each has contact with thousands and thousands of other systems during a lifetime. So collectively, there are millions and millions of interconnecting systems acting upon one another, giving rise to an infinite number of mutations in individual experiences, awarenesses, thoughts, and feelings.

The human brain is capable of an untold number of neurological transactions per second, making human thought processes extremely complex. Human thought is spontaneous, adaptive, ever-changing, and unpredictable, giving rise to ideas and opinions that are varied and divergent. They can evolve suddenly and impetuously or slowly and deliberately. They can appear random and scattered or orderly and coherent. Despite their content or origin, thoughts dynamically seek structure and order; we rationalize what we don't understand, we justify what we choose to believe, and we marginalize what we don't accept. This allows us to very quickly compartmentalize those things we believe to be right from those we believe to be wrong, those we believe to be good from those we believe to be bad. This provides each of us with unique perspectives that make our decisions feel logical, rational and, of course, "right."

Fertilization. Similar to the human fertilization process, perspectives evolve organically. They travel a journey much like the millions of sperm that are released during preconception. In the quest to fertilize a single egg, most sperm survive the hazardous journey through the female genital tract only to be blocked by the protective membrane of the egg created following fertilization by another sperm. Following fertilization, a series of events leads to the first cell division. A single-cell embryo is formed and subsequently undergoes multiple cell divisions during the process of mitosis. Mitosis ultimately transforms the embryo into a mass of very organized cells that eventually evolve into human form.

Origination. Consider the millions of spermatozoa to be the sum total of all our life experiences (for metaphoric purposes only). Let each sperm cell with its characteristically unique DNA structure represent one of those experiences. Think of the egg as the human mind, fertile ground for the sperm to be planted, be nourished and grow. However, the egg has a limited capacity to support the implantation of sperm—it's one and out. Similarly, the mind also has a limited ability to capture and retain experiences. Consequently, only some of those experiences will stand the test of time. In fertilization, only one sperm cell is able to penetrate the protective outer membrane of the egg. In life, only a select few pieces of data from our experiences finds a secure place in our long-term psyche. Like the sperm that fertilizes the egg, the data we take from experiences becomes the seed that when implanted in our minds supports the generation of other thoughts and ideas.

What plants. So the question is, "With all the experiential data we collect throughout our lives, what determines the data we choose to hold on to?" The answer is, "I don't have a clue!" Just like the millions of sperm that seek to fertilize a single egg, the combination of factors that allows one to be successful and the others to fail is a mystery to me. I'll leave that up to those who are eminently more qualified than I am. But in the absence of that knowledge, I'll do what I often do: make it up (like you don't). I'm going to say that the "strongest" sperm cell wins the race. This begs the question, what would determine the "strongest" cell? The answer to this one is, "It depends." (I know, not much better than "I don't have a clue.") But wait, there's more. It depends on a series of "environmental" factors that are random and unpredictable. So it requires an "if ...then... else" analysis, where there are an unlimited number of "if" conditions, an unlimited number of "then" conditions, and an unlimited number of "else" conditions. (What?) Let me explain. During the now-infamous journey of the sperm cell, it may encounter a number of different obstacles. For example, many don't get out of the starting blocks. Some can't survive the acidity at entry. Many get trapped by the cervix. Some get through the cervix but get lost in the mucus, etc. So it's almost impossible to anticipate whether any given cell will make it because of the ever-changing and unpredictable nature of the path along which they have to travel.

What roots. Similarly, the memories we retain from life experiences travel an equally perilous journey. These memories are usually a combination of facts and fantasy. And over time, the facts often become indistinguishable from the fantasy. How many times have you shared an experience with someone, after which they asked you about something of which you have no recollection (e.g., what someone said, did, saw). This just shows that some parts of every experience are obscure to us even when we experience them. It just doesn't register as worthy of attention. Some parts of the experience are noticed but never really take root. They go into a temporary mental file and are eventually discarded. While still other data, having more personal relevance, becomes like the sperm cell that fertilizes the egg; it becomes the one that takes root. Why? Because of the "personal relevance" thing, meaning it has a special connection to an individual's personal interests, values, or aspirations. Thus, "personal relevance" is the thing that is uncertain and unpredictable, and the "X" factor that determines whether something qualifies to be retained in our basket of trusted and reliable information. The storyteller retains and shares what they perceive to be relevant, as does the hearer. But what each finds relevant isn't always the same.

What grows. Once a "personally relevant" part of an experience finds its way into our long-term memory, it doesn't just lie dormant. Like the fertilized egg, it begins to divide and multiply. It becomes the standard we use to judge, interpret, take in, and make sense of our thoughts and actions and those of others.

What lives. Rationalizations, justifications, and marginalizations are all manifestations of our human need to give structure, order, and normalcy to our thoughts, feelings, and perceptions. All share characteristics with any number of ways we seek to make sense out of our life experiences.

Like the fertilization process, the human mind is bombarded with an untold number of sensations during the course of a lifetime. However, like the thousands of sperm that don't survive the race to fertilization, only a select few beliefs reach fertile ground, form roots, and are nurtured and allowed to mature. The others are often relegated to extinction. The sensations that ultimately survive and reach maturity form the foundation for our unique views of the world.

Views of the World

Where did the following line come from? "There are eight million stories in the naked city. This has been one of them." Of course it was the late '50's police drama series the *Naked City*. That simple statement expressed the boundless nature of human stories. Not only does everyone have *a* story, they actually have many. The narrative stories that we create give our lives a sense of meaning and purpose. Scientists say that our minds are more inclined to be story creators than logic processors. Rather than using logic to understand, we create stories to explain our life experiences.

Stories are generally simplified and selective reconstructions of things from our past that form the foundation for present thoughts and understandings. They are the thoughts, understandings, and beliefs that drive today's passions, decisions, and actions. They are the dreams and fantasies that reflect the hopes, wants, and desires for the future. These stories are a part of the very fabric of our lives. They influence our behaviors, our relationships, and even our mental health. They obviously have a huge impact on how we see ourselves but, more importantly, how we experience the world. These stories are the filters through which we make choices.

Stories can energize, but they can also demoralize. They can lift up, but they can also tear down. They can engage, but they can also alienate. They can empower but also debilitate. Given the profound impact that stories can have on how we not only view the world but, more importantly, how we engage in it, I have some thoughts on storytelling that I think will help us understand and leverage the power of stories.

Why is it that we can participate in the same event (for instance, read the same book, see the same movie, attend the same meeting, or go to the same class) yet experience them quite differently (like/dislike, good/bad, right/wrong, etc.)? Truly a mystery of life for God to know and man to ponder. Each of us is like a flake of snow, unique in size, shape, and structure. Beyond the physical, we have the added dimensions of personalities and beliefs. We all see the world differently. So when we read a book, see a movie, or attend a meeting, we experience them uniquely because of our different views of the world. We can see a glass of water as half empty or half full, a mere thirst quencher, or an essential ingredient of healthy bodily functions, a contributor to plant growth, or a driver of the universal climate system, or all of the above (or none of the above). Depending on its availability, we can see water opportunistically as a commodity or altruistically as a gift for all. I'm sure if we thought about it, we could think of a few (million) other ways to think about water. Who knew there were so many?

So the question is, why are there so many views of something as simple as water? I don't have a clue. I know you were waiting for some unbelievable insight, but unfortunately, "clueless" is all I got. But I feel quite comfortable saying that I have a lot of company. As a matter of fact, I think I would view someone who said they knew with certainty what someone else thought and why they thought it with more than a little skepticism. It's purely a conjecture game at best. We can, and do, come up with all kinds of explanations for why others think, say, and act as they do. But it's all "story." Unless we are highly intuitive, I mean hyper-to-the-max intuitive (omniscient if you will). I would say that it's difficult for us to even understand why we think and act the way we do. That's why psychiatry is such a lucrative profession.

The question that I always ask myself is, where did my "sparkling" personality and "impeccable" values come from? Was I born with all this goodness? Did I learn it from my parents or (God forbid) my friends? Was I just an astute observer of the world, or did I learn everything through osmosis? Once again, I'm clueless.

However, I'm thankful for people who are much brighter than I could ever hope to be, such as social psychologist Jonathan Haidt. Dr. Haidt said in his book *Righteous Mind* that "genes contribute, somehow to just about every aspect of our personalities." (Genes? Who would have thought—I was born with this stuff.) However, genes don't provide an explanation for all our personality, but apparently, they do have a greater influence on attitude and personality than one might think. It turns out that, according to Dr. Haidt, a predisposition to the types of food we eat, the kind of music we like, the kind of art we appreciate, and the level of religious affiliation—can have some origins in our DNA. Wow!

Genetic traits create little personalities right out of the womb? I always thought that babies were blank slates with no predispositions. I thought that every aspect of personality evolved over time as a result of their uniquely different life experiences. I thought that the adults that we became were a direct result of the lives we lived—*nurture* versus *nature*. It turns out that those cute little creatures that we bring into this world, adore in their innocence, and fawn over excessively (at least until they say "no!" the first time—and mean it) have the seeds of creation, destruction, production—already in them at birth. (How many of you would pay big money if there was a credible test to determine the innate preferences of your newborn child? (I, for one, wouldn't want to know. I think it's best that some things, like a child's personality, remain a mystery to be discovered versus a dilemma to be managed.) Dr. Haidt goes on to say that though certain personality traits have "innate" origins, innate doesn't mean rigid, unchanging, or unmalleable. His definition of innate is simply "organized in advance of experience." This seems to imply that instead of being a blank slate, babies are born with a "first draft" of who they will become. The seeds have already been planted and will ultimately be fed, nurtured, and modified by the experiences of life.

So what happens to those cute little baby brains over the span of their life that transform some of them into the cautious, reckless, cynical, idealistic, empathic, self-righteous adults that they ultimately become?

Dr. Haidt references a theory developed by Dr. Dan McAdams, professor and chair of the Department of Psychology at Northwestern University (Yahoo—Go Wildcats!) and author of *The Person: An Introduction to the Science of Personality Psychology.* Dr. McAdams asks, from scientific or psychological perspective, what do we know when we know a person?

Dr. McAdams theorizes that there are three levels of "knowing": dispositional traits, characteristic adaptations, and narrative identity.

The first level of "knowing" a person is through their "dispositional traits." These are considered the "lowest" dimension of personality and reflect a person's general tendencies such as how shy, outgoing, intelligent, or warm a person is. These traits seem to remain fairly consistent throughout a person's life. All these are present to varying degree in everyone. Dr. McAdams uses five broad factors to categorize personalities: (1) openness (curiosity or willing to try new things), (2) conscientiousness (self-discipline or self-control), (3) extraversion (approach to engaging the outside world), (4) agreeableness (the ability to get along with others), and (5) neuroticism (emotional instability). By the way, I struck out in all five categories. My self-assessment revealed that I was closed, undisciplined, extraverted, disagreeable and neurotic—which makes me a perfect candidate for political office (just a joke—on second thought, maybe not).

Moving to the second level increases our sense of "knowing" another person. This level is called "characteristic adaptations" and offers a more nuanced sense of a person's desires, beliefs, and concerns, as well as their approach to coping with the world at large. At this level, we gain insights into an individual's personal concerns, their strivings, life tasks, strategies of defense, coping mechanisms, and similar matters that involve the specific times, places, and endeavors of the person's life. These adaptations evolve in response to environmental challenges. They are reflected in influences, interests, preferences, choices, and decisions and drive the formation of different social, political, and moral themes. They speak to what people want and what life methods people use (strategies, plans, defenses, etc.) to get what they want or avoid getting what they don't want.

The third level of personality is called "narrative identity." People create an identity through a process Dr. McAdams calls "selfing," or describing our personalities by weaving together stories that define who we are. Selfing satisfies the need to answer the question "Who am I?" People construct somewhat coherent, understandable, and animated stories of themselves that describe their place in society. That is, people simply construct stories of themselves to convey who they are (e.g., a little of my story, "I was born by the river in a little tent. Just like the river I've been running ever since. It's been a long, a long time coming, but I know a change gonna come"—oh, I'm sorry; I got confused—that was Sam Cooke's story).

My story goes like this: "From very humble beginnings in a small town in Louisiana, I migrated north with my family at a very early age. I attended West Aurora High School, where I excelled in both academics and athletics. I decided to forego a possibly lucrative college basketball career to concentrate on more salient academic pursuits. After a very successful college experience, I was hired by a major international corporation, where I quickly rose through the ranks into leadership. I later left my corporate position for the opportunity to lead a mission-driven community-based organization. After which, I became an independent business consultant and a member of a prestigious international organizational development collective. My diverse life experiences have made me an astute observer of the environment around me—elevating my sense of awareness and appreciation for the nuances therein." (Sounds a lot like many résumés I've read—pure BS! Not a bad thing, just BS.)

Let's take a moment to analyze my *life story*.

Total BS	Less BS
"From very humble beginnings in small town Louisiana…"	I was born in a three-room house in Alexandria, Louisiana to teen parents who had a modest income which was close to, if not below, poverty level.
"I migrated north with my family at a very early age…"	When I was nine years old, we relocated to Aurora, Illinois, where I attended Beaupre Grade School and Franklin Junior High School.
"I attended West Aurora High School, where I excelled in both academics and athletics…"	I attended West Aurora High School, where I was an A/B student and a member of the National Honor Society. I was a starting guard on my high school basketball team.
"I decided to forego a possibly lucrative college basketball career to concentrate on more salient academic pursuits…"	I received inquiries from a couple of Division II/III schools that offered possible limited scholarship/financial support. I did attend a state-supported university with the aid of a scholarship from the Aurora Foundation.
"After a very successful college experience…"	I graduated from college with a bachelor of science degree in mathematics.
"I was hired by a major international corporation…"	I was hired by a major insurer as a programmer trainee two months after graduating from college.
"…where I quickly rose through the ranks into leadership."	I worked for twenty-nine years for a major insurance company, during which time I worked in three divisions—Information Technology, Financial Planning, and Human Resource Development. During my tenure, I also earned an MBA in finance.
"I later left my corporate position for the opportunity to lead a mission-driven community-based organization…"	I spent six years as executive director of a small not-for-profit.

"After which, I became an independent business consultant…"	I was an independent OD (organization development) consultant.
"…and a member of a prestigious international organizational development collective."	I completed the GESTALT International Organization and Systems Development Training Program.
"My diverse life experiences have made me an astute observer of the environment around me—elevating my sense of awareness and appreciation for the nuances therein…"	Pure unadulterated BS—yet a sincere expression of my firmly held belief. Not a lot of fact, but a whole lot of feel.

This bears an uncanny resemblance to Peter Senge's right-hand column / left-hand column that he presented in his book *The Fifth Discipline*. Senge used a two-column model to analyze tough communication issues that many of us would ignore given the choice. The first time I used this approach, the problem was so intense I didn't even want to write down in private what I was truly thinking. But in the long run, an honest assessment was exactly what was needed for me to reach any kind of concrete resolution.

In Senge's model, the right-hand column represents *what was said* during a problem exchange between you and someone else. These are the actual words that were used without censorship. Or if the conversation hasn't occurred yet, then you can write down the dialogue as you think it might play out if you were to raise this issue. Play this construed dialogue all the way out based on what you know (or think you know) of the other person.

Once you've completed the dialogue in the right column, it's time to move to the left-hand column. In this column, Senge asks you to write down *what you were thinking but not saying* as the dialogue in the right-hand column was taking place. This is no time for PC (political correctness). I've always been taught that "the truth will set you free." This is the hard part—being brutally honest with yourself. I was totally surprised at the level of emotion that lay just below the surface. I learned a great deal by reviewing what I had written. I was able to more thoroughly examine my own thinking, as though

I were analyzing the words and thoughts of someone else. It was liberating! The next step for me, which most people familiar with this approach aren't willing to do, is to share the left-hand column with the others involved. Though I have to admit that on the occasions, when I shared my left column, I often had to do some minor editing to remove any offensive or otherwise inappropriate language without losing the integrity of what I was thinking.

Total BS

My two columns represent a kind of "reverse" Senge model. The left column I call *total BS*. If you go back and read the left column of my life story, you'll notice that the statements are dominated more by thoughts and feelings than specific events and occurrences. I used phrases like "*humble beginnings*," "*excelled* in both academics and athletics*," "*successful* college experience," "*prestigious* international organization collective," "*astute* observer the environment around me," and "*elevating my sense of awareness and appreciation.*"

Each of these phrases includes some implicit value or standard that may or may not be shared by others. For instance, a simple phrase like "humble beginnings" seems so straightforward, yet it holds so much meaning in my heart. Whereas *humble* usually implies a person of modest means or low social status. For me, it meant oh so much more. It brings back memories of parental sacrifice, of appreciation and thankfulness for the simple things in life. It conjures up thoughts of compassion and empathy for those having even less than my family, of the value and importance of relationships in creating a joyful environment, and much, much more. Unlike some who might view "humble beginnings" with sympathy, I think about humble beginnings with a true sense of pride.

That "lucrative college basketball career" thing may be a bit of an exaggeration. In high school, I probably averaged 8 points, 3 rebounds, and 2 assists per game. Mediocre by most high school performance standards. But the thing I took pride in was my defensive abilities. In fact, I was known as a defensive specialist and was usually assigned to the leading scorer on the opposing team. (Just a note to any college or pro scouts out there looking for a somewhat seasoned guard, I still have my Converse All Stars in the closet ready to go. Call me.) Anyway, following high school, I played well enough in intramural, playground pickup, and summer league basketball to convince myself that I could have played college basketball if I wanted to. My story was, if I had just accepted those division II school offers, played two years, and then transferred to a division I school, who knows, I could have been in the NBA today. Not!

Did you notice the difference in the two stories? The first story has been very inspirational in my life. Every time I think about it, it makes me think about my parents and my core values. The second story was aspirational. I think about how dedicated and disciplined I was about being in shape and prepared for the basketball season (I even ran cross-country. And believe me, it wasn't for the joy of running). At that time, I aspired to be the best player I could be with the hope of some future opportunities.

Jonathan Haidt calls these stories "simplified and selective reconstructions of the past, often connected to an idealized vision of the future." Translation—they're some made-up BS. They had simple beginnings, evolved over time, served a specific purpose when they were created, have personal meaning, and though not "true" in the purest sense of the word, reflect a personalized construct of "the truth" as I know it.

Less BS

Now moving to the right column. I have chosen to call the right column *less BS*. It's easy to see the obvious difference between the content of the right and left columns. While the left column reflects more thoughts and feelings, the right column contains the actual events and occurrences behind them. The right column is more data intensive—leaving less room for personal judgment. Hence, less BS.

Less BS leaves less room for judgment. However, less judgment doesn't mean "no" judgment. Though the events themselves are factual, deciding which events to choose opens the door to our biases. For example, I used "graduated from college with a Bachelor of Science (BS) in Mathematics" to substantiate a "very successful college career." What if I had said instead, "I was placed on academic probation my freshman year after falling behind in several core math classes due to absenteeism, and again my junior year after having to drop several classes in which I was performing poorly"? (Just in case Moms and Pops are reading this, the "probation thing" never happened!) But what if I had only shared the probation thing, would you think that my college career had been successful? Probably not. You might have come up with a number of other descriptions of my college experience, like, "irresponsible," "undisciplined," "inconsistent," "mediocre," and "lucky," but certainly not "successful."

If you look only at the content of the less BS column, your own thoughts, feelings, and preferences will undoubtedly come into focus. Without the descriptive phrase "successful college career" (from the total BS column), "bachelor in science in mathematics" might become the dominant focus of attention. Depending on your predilection for mathematics, you might think, "That's a really hard major," or, "You must be really logical and detail-minded," or, "All those math theories and formulas have little value in the real world." These thoughts would become the foundation for, perhaps, a different story. Rather than a "successful" college career, you might think it must have been a "challenging," "productive," or "impractical" college career.

Looking at both columns, you may also feel that the events and occurrences listed in the less BS column don't necessarily align with the descriptions in the total BS column. For instance, in your mind, the "twenty-nine years" (in the less BS column) may not substantiate the statement "I quickly rose through the ranks into leadership" (as expressed in the total BS column). However, what if I added to the less BS column "I received ten promotions, five staff-level and five leadership-level positions in the first fifteen years, with the first leadership position achieved within the first five years of employment, three years earlier than the corporate average. After which, I rotated as an executive to three different major corporate divisions: Information Technology, Financial Planning, and Human Resource?" Would that make a difference?

Compound BS

Data always gives a story more flavor. But data can be used to intentionally validate or discredit a story. The greater the amount of data, the greater the opportunity for someone to selectively use that data to create an alternative story. Thus the emergence of *compound BS*.

So if you're trying to convince someone of the righteousness of your perspective, you would probably stick with a high level "story" rather than sharing any relevant detail. For instance, politicians will usually tell you "what" they'll do rather than "how" they'll do it—I'll feed the poor, clothe the naked, improve the economy, defeat the enemy, save the planet if you'll just vote for me (total BS). When questioned further on how they will do all these wonderful things, or perhaps what have they done related to these things in the past, their responses will probably contain either more empty platitudes or quickly shift to the shortcomings of their opponents—anything to avoid providing more detail on what they would actually do. Some politicians don't even take a shot at a reasonable response to the question of "how" but skillfully shift the conversation from one of strategy to one of relationship (e.g., "I can be trusted, but my opponent can't").

But if you try to convince someone of the strength of your position, then data becomes your friend. For instance, if you were a politician who wanted to convince the public that you are operating from a position of knowledge and experience, you might move toward less BS. Rather than just saying "I will improve the state of our economy," you might provide your measures for evaluating the health of the economy, an assessment of various economic indicators, and a specific strategy for achieving any targeted results. Of course, this would leave you much more open to the *creative respinning* or *compound BS-ing* of your story by others. They would probably go over each element of your strategy in meticulous detail, taking every opportunity to highlight and label component parts of your story as "ridiculous," "outrageous," "naive," "ill-informed," or "stupid." It could be the most brilliant offering possible, and you could be the most qualified person to make it happen, yet it would still be met with the same level of denigration. Consequently, it's much easier (and probably much more effective with some segments of the community) to say "the economy is screwed up"—whether it's a statement of fact or not—"and I'll fix it"—whether they're qualified to do so or not.

So you can see how BS can be a much more useful tool for moving public opinion. However, less BS can be a much more useful tool for defining real problems and pursuing concrete solutions. Both can be useful to politicians. If they simply want to make an emotional appeal (heart), a lot of detail probably wouldn't work. However, if they want to make a rational appeal (mind), a certain amount of data would probably be advantageous. *Though everyone responds to both emotional and logical appeals, the challenge is finding the appropriate balance of each for the audience you're addressing.*

I've often heard that you should never discuss religion or politics. These are areas of BS that most will steer away from because of the intensity of the personal convictions and the unyielding emotional attachment some might have to their underlying beliefs. This creates the potential for volatility anytime these topics are brought up. I've seen calm and rational discussions quickly erupt into emotional chaos when the wrong button is accidently pushed. This may be fueled by our fear or just downright defiance to having our worldviews questioned or examined? This can make it challenging for some to speak openly even to friends about these highly controversial topics and come out on the other end still friends. I ask that you pause for a minute and think about where you stand on discussing your most strongly held BS. Do you feel that your BS can stand up to the scrutiny of others? Do you get offended when others challenge your BS? Or do you defensively offer knowingly "invalid" information to justify your BS?

Before we go any further, for some, the following subjects may fall in the "taboo topic tub." However, not being one to shy away from a lively exchange, I'm going to go there anyway. I only ask that you proceed with a conscious level of neutrality, indifference, and intellectual curiosity (in other words, don't get upset).

So speaking of religion and politics, how about those Chicago Bulls? (Just a momentary diversion before getting into the meat of what I want to really say.) Now, where was I?

Those who read the Bible know that Bible messages are often shared through proverbs, riddles, and parables. These are essentially stories that are designed to teach a basic truth or moral value. Many have attacked the credibility of such stories based on the facts as they are presented. One highly controversial example is the story of Jonah and the whale.

In the story, Jonah was ordered by God to go to the city of Nineveh to warn them of the consequences of their wicked ways. Instead, Jonah attempted to flee against God's will and encountered a huge storm while traveling by sea. The crew of the ship transporting Jonah realized that the storm was no ordinary storm. They blamed Jonah, who readily admitted his culpability and informed the sailors that the storm would cease if they just threw him (Jonah) overboard. The sailors eventually complied and threw him overboard. The sea was immediately calmed. As the story goes, Jonah was then miraculously saved by being swallowed by a whale that had been sent by God. He is said to have spent three days and three nights inside the whale. While in the whale, Jonah prayed to God and recommitted to paying what he had vowed. God then commanded the mammal to vomit Jonah out. Jonah was once again ordered to go and prophesize to the people of Nineveh. This time he did as he had been instructed. God mercifully spared the city after its inhabitants humbly responded to the message delivered by Jonah.

People respond to this well-known biblical story in a number of different ways. One, some who strongly believe in the literal interpretation of the Bible may say that if it's in the Bible, it is historically and factually accurate—no if, ands or buts. Two, others may say that this is a parable that teaches the spiritual lessons of obedience, gratitude, and compassion. Three, others may say that it's remotely possible, but highly unlikely that a whale could swallow a man whole, let alone that man could survive inside a whale for three days. Four, still others may say that the story is ridiculous and not even worthy of consideration.

If you go back and view the small sampling of possible responses, you'll see that they are all a mixed bag of *facts* and *beliefs*.

- The person that questions whether a whale could swallow a man whole is focused on the *facts* of the story and their *belief* (or even studied knowledge) about a whale's capacity to swallow, and a man's ability to survive after being swallowed.
- The person that identifies the story as a parable is focused less on the literal *facts* of the story than on the *belief* that there are implicit lessons to be learned from the story.
- The person that accepts the literal interpretation of the Bible is focused only on the *fact* that it is "the Bible" and their strongly held *belief* in an unconditional acceptance of the events just as they are presented.
- The person who considers the story unworthy of consideration is not focused on the *facts* but on their *belief* that the situation is inconceivable or maybe even that the Bible is not credible.

As you can see, the *focus* of each of the perspectives is different. From a Gestalt perspective, each person focuses on a different "figure"—the Bible itself, the meaning of the Bible's parables, the whale, and the Bible's credibility. The *beliefs* that are identified are related to the "figure" that each has chosen to focus on. So if any two of these people were having a conversation about the story, it's highly possible, and indeed probable, that they would be focusing on completely different things, justifying their own BS by refuting that of others without realizing that it's all BS.

Section 2: It's Complicated

- ❖ Origins of belief systems
  - ➤ The human brain is capable of an untold number of neurological transactions per second.

- ➢ Human thoughts are spontaneous, adaptive, ever-changing and unpredictable.
- ➢ Certain personality traits are "organized in advance of our experience" (Dr. Jonathan Haidt).
- ➢ Three dimensions of personality development (Dr. Dan McAdams).
  - o "Dispositional traits"—a person's general tendencies (i.e., shyness).
  - o "Characteristic Adaptations"—a person's desires, beliefs, concerns, and life approaches.
  - o "Narrative Identity"—the process of developing stories that reflect one's personal identity.

- ❖ Views of the World
  - ➢ Stories are generally simplified and selective reconstructions of things from our past (McAdams).
  - ➢ Stories are a combination of facts and beliefs.
  - ➢ Stories have both logical and emotional appeal.
  - ➢ Data can be used to either validate or discredit a story.
  - ➢ Facts are created from a systematic examination of relevant data.
  - ➢ What you think is often based more on what you believe than what is factual.
  - ➢ What you say is not always consistent with what you think.

III. Bias? What Bias?

Biases are everywhere. They are as pervasive in our lives as the air we breathe. We are not only inundated with them internally but saturated with them externally. Their origins can either be discrete or varied, their impact subtle or dynamic. Though they're not always obvious, they are indeed always present.

UNCONSCIOUS BIASES

stereotypes
hasty generalization
guilty by association
sexism   appeal to fear
bandwagon effect   racism
slippery slope fallacy
confirmation bias   prejudice
discrimination
herd mentality   hindsight bias
self-serving bias
backfire effect   anchoring
negativity bias

As previously discussed, most stories have an untold number of biases. These biases are often based more on familiarity than rationality. Familiarity being what we believe to be true and rationality what we can logically prove to be true. Harold Goddard once said, "The destiny of the world is determined…less by the battles that are lost and won than…by the stories it loves and believes in." Goddard seems to imply that biased stories, those we love and believe in, can not only impact our personal destiny, but indeed the destiny of the entire world.

Biased stories have incredible power. They can diminish our strengths, elevate our weaknesses, magnify our fears, dampen our joys, and otherwise distort our reality. This has a direct impact on how we see and engage with the world. If our worldview is that a certain race, religion, lifestyle is "bad," we may view it with contempt and respond to it accordingly. Since race, religion, and lifestyle are human constructs, they are inherently biased.

Biases are natural! Everyone has them whether they are aware of it or not. However, if you were to ask someone if they had any biases, most would adamantly proclaim "absolutely not," even if it was obvious to the rest of the world that they did. We all have some social, political, religious, or other identity-group bias. If we have biases, why do we not just claim them? Probably because there is a stigma attached to the word *biased*. After all, if you're biased, you can't possibly be open-minded, fair, impartial, and nonjudgmental.

And of course, we all want to believe that we are all these things. And we can't be these things if we are biased. Right?

I happen to be one of the few admittedly biased people in the world. I have a preference for Chicago over Los Angeles, basketball over baseball, scotch over gin, Snickers over Milky Way, and Coke over Pepsi. The more observant among you might have noticed that I substituted the word *preference* for *bias*. "I'm not biased. I just have a preference for…" But aren't they the same thing? Well, not exactly. Having a preference just means liking one thing more than another. However, having a bias generally implies that you prefer something, often unconsciously, based on a preexisting view, regardless of whether it's right or wrong. I can hear most of you thinking, "My preferences are not biased!" And they may not all be. But I would be willing to bet that many are.

Most stories have selective preferences based on what we believe to be true versus what may actually be true. They give favor or advantage to someone or something based purely on what we feel is right. The more intense the feeling, the greater the attachment. The greater the attachment, the higher the probability of thoughts and actions being positively or negatively influenced. The dark underside of these biases often shows up in religion and politics where one group may be given advantage or preferential treatment even though all are equally entitled.

The following are some common types of biases:

- *Confirmation bias* is a preference for perspectives that reinforce (confirm) what you already believe. (Ignores or diminishes opinions that are different from your world view.)
- *Selection bias* is a preference for facts that support your pre-existing beliefs. (Selection of data in a way that prevents proper randomization needed for sound judgment).
- *Expectancy bias* is a preference for results that support your expected outcome. (Interpreting results in favor of what you expected the results would be.)

- *Bandwagon bias* is a preference for opinions that you feel will create the least conflict or division. (Lacks critical evaluation; going along to get along.)
- *Opportunity bias* is a preference for one group over another that affords the preferred group unearned advantage. (Provides rewards and benefits based on arbitrary choice or differentiation.)

This is just a few of the many cognitive biases that exist.

Having a personal bias is not unusual. We all have some opinion on whether there are inequities in personal freedoms (e.g., religion, expression), opportunities (e.g., education, employment), protection (e.g., safety, property), or social security (e.g., medical access, affordable housing). It's not their existence that is problematic. It's how aware we are of our own and how we act on that awareness that matters. You can like Coke over Pepsi, but if you decide to shut down all Pepsi manufacturers because you like Coke, *you* have now limited *my* freedom, my access, and my choice. So it's not the preference but the unfair judgment that makes them biased and the resulting inequitable acts that make them dysfunctional.

Situational versus Cognitive Bias

Following is a series of brief narratives. As you read them, notice the content of each story and its component parts. There are situational elements like the people (the characters), the place (the environment), the interplay between characters, and the environment (the plot) that create the circumstances (the situation). All are necessary components of any story.

However, there are some elements that are not quite so obvious, like the dynamic tension that exits between the characters, the cause of that tension, and its ultimate resolution. These things are called cognitive elements. They reveal each character's thoughts, feelings, and motives. Most good fiction writers use these elements to optimize reader engagement.

I just finished reading a novel (whose title will remain anonymous for fear of your judgment of my literary taste) in which I was a captive until the very last few pages. I had already decided which characters I liked, those I didn't, those that were relevant, and those that weren't, and most importantly, I had figured out "who done it." And of course, you guessed it—I was wrong. Having read the novel first, I thought it was fun listening to my wife come up with all her theories about who did what and why. The interesting thing is that she came up with completely different theories than I did at the same point in the story—and of course, she was wrong too! (It's a good thing. I never would have heard the end of it had she been able to figure it out before me. BTW, she usually does. Anyway, where was I? Oh yeah, situational and cognitive elements.)

Each story also has a bias bent. Some of the biases are situational or circumstantial and others are cognitive—a product of the storyteller's own "subjective reality" or personal point of view. Note—though you may be able to find a number of other examples of bias in each story, I've chosen to isolate and focus on a few of the *situational biases* that I felt were at play.

*****

Confirmation Bias
Weasy, Queasy, and Uneasy

I didn't fly (at least in a plane) until the ripe old age of thirty-five, which was relatively late in life compared to most of my friends. Now you need to understand that I had a strongly held belief that flying wasn't safe long before my first flight, and ample evidence to support it, at least in my mind. After all, if God had meant for us to fly, he would have given us wings (I bet you've never heard that one before). Needless to say, I woke up the morning of my first flight with what I can only describe as a weasy, queasy, uneasy feeling, or somewhere between a bad case of vertigo and diarrhea.

Now I've heard that many people experience the condition known as glossophobia, an anxiety associated with public speaking.

I'm quite familiar with this condition since I've been its beneficiary on a number of occasions. Pteromerhanophobia (I can't pronounce it either), also known as aerophobia, is more commonly known as the fear of flying. I had a case of pteromerhanophobia that was so extreme that it was off the glossophobic charts. As a matter of fact, I would venture to guess that if you took my glossophobic fears, multiplied them by ten to the power of three plus one, you might still fall short of the angst I felt that day.

It just so happened that my first flight was also the first flight for my children, who were about ages four and six at the time. As you might suspect, they anticipated their first venture into the wild blue yonder with youthful exuberance and excitement. This created somewhat of a challenge for me. In order to be the pillar of strength, reassurance, and support that I felt my children needed, I had to project an aura of calm, unconcerned indifference, despite the volcanic-like angst bubbling up inside. I had to resist engaging in any action that might embarrass me and, more importantly my children—you know, like demanding the pilot land the plane somewhere fifty thousand feet over Tulsa—or at least let me off.

I actually don't know where this almost debilitating fear of flying came from. It might have been an unintended byproduct of my mother's fear, which prevented her from flying until relatively late in life. It could have been an impression that I got from friends after hearing their horror stories of business flights where they encountered excessive turbulence, severe drops in altitude, and even aborted landings. It might have been just something I created in my own little head based on something as innocuous as the light-headedness I often felt when looking down from high places, like my first glimpse down from atop the Grand Canyon, which was awesomely terrifying. But in the moment, where it came from wasn't important.

My only focus then was the fact that it was slapping me in the face with increasing intensity. As I boarded the plane, I thought about how Joan of Arc might have felt knowing that her demise was imminent. I shot up a quick prayer before crossing the plane's threshold—the point of no return. I slowly and reluctantly sauntered down the narrow aisle. With each advancing step, I had to resist the urge to turn around and charge the exit, annihilating all that blocked the path between me and the door to freedom. As I gently maneuvered my way down the aisle, trying to avoid inadvertently assaulting those who happened to be seated along the aisle with my overweight carryon bag, it struck me how calm everyone else seemed to be. In fact, as I looked around, there were several people who were already reading books, looking at their smart phones (I hope they were in flight mode). Some even appeared to be sleep—or perhaps they had fainted from their fear and were unknowingly in a petrified state. But at the moment, I couldn't concern myself with them. I had problems of my own. In just a matter of moments, we were going to be launched down the runway and hurled into the air at warp speed? What was wrong with these people—how could they be so casual and unassuming?

I listened attentively to the flight attendant's preflight instructions. How do I find that damn flotation device that she said was somehow attached to my seat? I know that inquiring minds wanted to know, but desperate minds needed to know! Since no one else seemed very interested, I didn't want to be the only one to raise my hand with a question. But I had a lot of questions following the somewhat uninspired, inadequate, and less than enthusiastic presentation given by the flight attendant.

As instructed, I read the in-flight pocket guide from cover to cover—twice. I looked over at the kids, who still appeared to be in a state of euphoric anticipation. I flashed them what I hoped was a reassuring smile as I checked their seat belts to make sure they were securely strapped in. At this point, I decided to settle in and try to enjoy the flight. That lasted about five minutes until the plane turned onto the designated runway for takeoff and immediately began accelerating. A final prayer for traveling mercy, a quick glance at the kids, and we were off.

As the plane began to climb, I was sensitive to the slightest roll and bank as it positioned itself for the ultimate climb to cruising altitude. I noticed every sound—the retracting of the landing gear, the changing pitch of the engine as it alternately accelerated and decelerated—and other sounds that I had no idea of their source.

I keyed in on the flight attendant who was in clear sight, looking for the slightest change in her expression (surely she would give me the best indication as to whether any of these sensations that I was experiencing for the first time were out of the norm). I responded to each new motion and sound with a tightening of my already-firm grip on the armrest, as though it was some magic lever that would activate some sort of escape capsule if the plane, God forbid, happened to encounter some sort of distress. I actually discovered the meaning of "white knuckle" flying that day. I had subconsciously gripped the armrest so tight during the early flight that I had partially cut off the circulation in my hands, which I didn't realize until I had once again (with all gratitude and thanksgiving) reached terra firma.

Once the plane reached cruising altitude and leveled off, which seemed an eternity, the next thing I knew, the beverage cart appeared, and the flight attendant pleasantly inquired about my beverage choice. Once given, she graciously responded by not only giving me the beverage I requested, but also the added bonus of a snack (who cares that it was just fifteen peanuts in a logo-laden plastic package. It was the idea of that free, unexpected, and unsolicited little extra that has in all probability been banished from the annals of flight history forever. I remember thinking midflight, *Hm, only two hours to get to a place that normally takes me thirteen hours to drive—friendly flight attendants, free snacks, in-flight movie—this isn't half bad*. I might even consider doing this again (with the emphasis on "might").

Something I want to point out here is that we enter every experience with a certain amount of preexisting BS. That BS can either be the result of personal observations, information from what is believed to be a "credible" source, inferences drawn from a collection of random sources (e.g., books and other publications) or not directly related information, just an inference pulled from the cosmos of unrelated data.

Some stories, depending on how widely shared and accepted they are, become bigger than life. They become so entrenched in our beliefs and ingrained in our thinking that we stop challenging their validity. In essence, they stop being stories and morph into (drumroll please, *ta-da!) the truth*!

Our entire collection of BS that we've developed from child-hood to date becomes what I like to refer to as our "crockadoodle" (or "crock," for short). Think about it. A crock is an earthenware vessel or container, and a doodle is something of our own creation. Therefore, it's logical that a crockadoodle would be a container that holds matter of our own creation. In other words, a crockadoodle is a collection of BS that we have created from our experiences and hold to be true (possibly without substantiation or even with a significant body of evidence to the contrary). Our crockadoodle contains all forms of BS—that which is conceivable, believable, and undeniable.

Everyone has their own unique set of crockadoodles, filled with their own highly valued, personally chosen, and time-tested BS. Each crockadoodle is initially created to serve a specific purpose—to relieve a pain, satisfy a need, solve a problem, or explain a condition. Our collection of crockadoodles are the remnants of our past; they're what's left after the facts of our experiences have long since been cropped, redressed, and preserved for posterity. Any recall of these old stories are filled with the biases of our memory and may bear little or no resemblance to the actual experiences from which they originated. With each new experience we subconsciously seek to con-firm or reinforce the validity of our long-held collection of bias-based crockadoodles (confirmation bias). So, no matter what you think of the story of my first flight, flying isn't safe!

Selection Bias
The Same Experiences, Not Experienced the Same

My friend and professional colleague, Jay, and I once attended the presentation of a well-known author and expert in the field of leadership and collective intelligence. We were both extremely inter-ested in the topic and had been excitedly anticipating this presen-tation for weeks. You might be thinking "collective intelligence," "exciting," in the same sentence? Yes, we are indeed a different bunch of bananas. However, if this topic doesn't rock your boat, feel free to substitute the topic of your choice in place of "leadership and collec-tive intelligence" so you won't get left behind. Anyway, we (meaning me and he) were very excited. When we arrived, we discovered that a rather large number of others seemed to be excited as well. After a somewhat long and convoluted introduction, it was finally time for the main event. Onto the stage walks the object of our admiration, in the flesh. He immediately launches into a presentation that I can only describe as wow! I thought it was the most informative, insightful, and engaging discussion of (please fill in the topic of your choice here) that I had ever heard. He was all that and a bag of chips (for those of you who don't know, "a bag of chips" is a colloquialism for that something extra that you get that you didn't expect). I couldn't have been more pleased. Don't you just love it when that happens?

It turns out that not everyone was as enthusiastic about the presentation as I was (hard as that might be to imagine)—most notably, my dear friend, colleague, and presentation con padre, Jay. I noticed as we were exiting that Jay's expression was not one of joy and thanksgiving, as it should have been after hearing such a rousing presentation, but more akin to constipation (sorry, just my impression).

When I asked him what he thought, he responded, "That was one of the worst presentations I've ever experienced." After picking my lower lip up off the floor and regaining my composure from being blindsided by this unexpected response, I asked him with the most neutral tone and demeanor I could muster up, "Why did you think it was so bad?"—resisting the temptation to tell him how I really felt about his obviously irrational, and by the way flat-out "wrong," assessment.

Prepared to defend my sensei of collective intelligence to the death, Jay's response was surprisingly quite interesting. I had been so entranced by the subject matter and how it was presented that I hadn't even noticed some of the things that were so obviously important to Jay.

First, Jay pointed out that the amount of information on each slide and the smallness of the font made the slides practically useless as a visual aid. (Okay, one for Jay). Secondly, everything the presenter shared was totally theoretical with no examples or ways to practically apply it to anything. (A bit harsh from my perspective, but okay.) Thirdly, Jay said that the speaker, being a professed atheist, used what

Jay felt was a cynical reference to people of faith that he found totally offensive early in the presentation. (How had I missed that one?) Hm, visually challenging, missing examples of practical application, insensitive language—not a bad assessment from someone so obviously misguided, delusional, and wrong!

I was intrigued but not swayed by Jay's assessment (though, the perceived-slight-against-people-of-faith thing almost got me). As though I had been personally assaulted by Jay's attack on what had once been our unblemished guru of collective intelligence, in true superfan fashion, I came to my hero's defense. I had a few intellectually stimulating and provocative insights of my own. "But, Jay, didn't you see the suit he had on? You've got to give him style points. And did you hear that joke he made about... You've got to admit that was pretty funny. As a matter of fact, his sense of humor kept me engaged the entire time. And you know what else? He clarified the 'theory X' of collective intelligence that we've both been confused about for some time. Come on, Jay, you've got to give the man credit. He knows his stuff."

Jay just walked away with his eyes pointed due south and his head subtly moving east and west.

Of course, this isn't exactly the way it happened. I had deeper thoughts than the fashion worthiness of the presenter's suit. (In reality, I probably would have focused on something much more significant—like his shoes. Now they're important! You can tell a lot about a person by just checking out their shoes.) Anyway, the point is that each of us had different things that were important to us. These things stood out like neon signs—so bright that they just commanded our attention. They so dominated our focus that everything else paled in comparison. For Jay, it was the composition of the presenter's slides (he had been a graphic designer in a prior life), the practicality of the theory (which had been part of our shared dilemma), and most importantly, the perceived degrading comments about people of faith (Jay's father was a minister, and he had been active in the church all his life). For me, it was what I simply choose to refer to as style, smile, and profile. He had the style, he made me smile, and he maintained his credible profile (hero status still intact).

So all this might beg the question, "Who was right?" The obvious answer is me (because I'm always right—at least in my head). But I'm sure Jay was equally adamant about the righteousness of his perspective.

There's a distinction that I think is important to make here. "Right" is often viewed in a lot of different ways. There is a rationally based perspective around rightness as well as an emotional perspective. The rational perspective focuses more on the accuracy and correctness of the information used, commonly referred to as the "facts." The emotional dimension focuses more on the conclusions that you draw either from the facts, or heaven forbid, no facts at all. The latter, of course, is more interpretive than factual.

I want to once again emphasize how we uniquely experience things. When Jay pointed out the font size on the slides, the missing practical application of the theory, and the speaker's seemingly negative reference to people of faith, I was able to connect with every one of his observations. Jay even agreed with me about the speaker's style (the suit really was exceptional), his sense of humor, and knowledge of the subject. But by pointing them out, we (1) made them "hyper-visible" to the other person and (2) shared them in a way that caused the other person to see them differently.

Making something visible to someone else that may have previously gone unnoticed is called making that something "figural." That just means that it elevates and differentiates it from everything else around it (the environment). The second part, causing others to see that thing differently, would be called creating new "awareness," which essentially means allowing someone to see that particular thing again, but in a different light. The "figure-awareness" language is from Gestalt methodology and may be new to many of you. But as you can see, it can be an important concept in helping us understand why we see things so differently.

In the now-infamous James-and-Jay experience, we saw how focusing on different facts, even though the same experience, can lead to completely different perspectives. Each of these perspectives says something about the person who creates them—what they feel is important and what they believe to be true. Each person hears, understands, and defines the meaning of each "story" in their own unique way.

With James and Jay, we were able to observe the construction of each of their differing perspectives from "soup to nuts." We were able to see what facts they used, how they interpreted those facts, and what stories they ultimately created. But most exchanges aren't that transparent or easy to follow. We generally only see the end product of a subtly integrated and complex thought process. In the case of James and Jay, that end product was two competing perspectives that were polar opposites: one believing the presentation "was the most informative, insightful, and engaging" they had ever seen and the other that it was "one of the worst presentations" they had ever seen. Each reflecting a uniquely biased view of the limitless and dynamic tapestry of the world we live in.

Consider for a moment the number of things that James and Jay could have focused on—the presenter (e.g., knowledge, enthusiasm, appearance, and responsiveness), the presentation (e.g., organization, delivery, clarity, conciseness, practicality), the audience (e.g., excitement, engagement, participation, disruption), the environment (e.g., impact, size, seating, décor) and numerous others. Now assume that there were three hundred people in the audience—randomly reacting to any or all of the aforementioned elements. How many different observations might have been made about the same element? How many of those observations might have been the same, different, or seemingly the same but for different reasons? How many stories do you think might have been created collectively by the group? Obviously too many to count, let alone to know and understand. Our differing *expectations* drove each of us to create differing stories.

Expectancy Bias
A Cautionary Tale

A feedback story that I heard early in life was the biblical story of David, king of the United Kingdom of Israel and Judah, and Bathsheba. As many of you know, Bathsheba was originally the wife of a Hittite soldier named Uriah. The story is told that David, while walking on the roof of his palace, saw Bathsheba, the wife of Uriah, bathing. He was immediately smitten by her. And since he was king, having all power over his domain, he was able to indiscriminately act on his desires without consequence, which he did. This eventually led to Bathsheba's impregnation.

In an effort to conceal this immoral deed, David summoned Uriah from the battlefield in the hope that he would resume marital relations with Bathsheba so he would think that the child Bathsheba was carrying was his. Uriah, being the consummate soldier, chose not to violate the ancient warrior code of conduct for active service members and remained with the palace troops. After repeated attempts to get Uriah to have sex with Bathsheba, the king gave the order to his general that Uriah should be placed on the front lines of the battlefield, where it was the most dangerous. According to David's plan, Uriah would be killed in battle. After Uriah's death, David would then take the widowed Bathsheba as his wife.

Now the prophet Nathan enters the picture. He had the unenviable task of approaching the king about his extreme acts of indiscretion. I think here we need a little context about the despotic rule of kings at the time. They ruled with absolute power. By absolute, I mean with unlimited power—with no restrictions or boundaries. There were no systems of checks and balances or governing standards of right or wrong, good or bad, just or unjust—the king's word was final. Consequently, as in King David's case, there were frequent abuses of power. This obviously significantly raised the level of risk associated with Nathan's task. Depending on the king's temperament that day, Nathan could be opening himself up to anything from a mild reprimand to a horrible, horrible death.

Let's pause for a minute and think about how we might have approached Nathan's challenge? If it were me, it might have gone something like this: "Oh almighty, benevolent, merciful, and caring king, protector of the downtrodden, the pentacle of wisdom and power, the purveyor of truth and justice, I beseech you grant me a moment of your precious time." Too much? Maybe. I'm certainly not an advocate of insincere or excessive praise. But I do believe in the power of sincere affirmation and, more importantly, self-preservation. That "risk of death" thing might cause some insincerity to creep in. (Oh, like you always say exactly what you think. Right. Anyway, let's continue.)

"Dear king, I wish to revisit the dispensation of the case of Uriah the Hittite." Bet that would get his attention. It's not like he won't remember Uriah, since he had a living reminder in the form of his ex-wife in the next room. At this point depending on the king's mood, there might be an abrupt end to the conversation, not to mention my life. However, let's assume that the king is in a curious mood and allows me to continue.

In my head, I might want to say, "Okay, king, just between you and me, you know what you did to Uriah was wrong. You put the poor man on the frontline of the battlefield, knowing he would be killed, just so you could cover up the dirty deed you did with his wife. You, I and everybody else knows that ain't right. Come on now, king. What's up with that?" But there was something in the king's expression and tone at the mere mention of Uriah's name that caused me to rethink this before sharing it openly. It came out something like this, "Uriah was a good and honorable man who died in your service. I'm sure he would be grateful for the loving kindness you've shown his surviving widow. We, your loyal subjects, are indeed grateful to have such a benevolent king." Not quite what I was thinking. But surely the king would be reminded of his role in Uriah's death and feel some sense of remorse. Maybe not. What he might feel is anger and resentment directed at me for bringing up a subject that he had conveniently buried in the recesses of his memory, never ever, ever to be thought of, let alone spoken of again. Maybe this was not such a good idea.

Let's assume that the king has been sufficiently "snowed" by my diversionary tactics that he miraculously allows me to continue. What could I say that would get him to see the error of his ways without igniting the fire of his wrath? Okay, it's now or never. I'm going to tell the king what I came here to tell him. Okay, how do I do this? Oh I know, I'll wow him with a rhyme. "Mary had a little ewe…" No, how about a song. "I only have eyes for ewe…" No, no. How about a riddle. "There once was a poor man named Uriah—I mean Jeremiah…" No, no, no. I know what I'll do. I'll just stick with the facts. Yea, that's it—the facts. So I lift my head, square my shoulders, and take a deep breath and say, "Your Majesty, I just wanted to know where you think I should forward the meager belongings that Uriah had on his person at the time of his demise. He is only survived by his beloved widow, Bathsheba, who is now a member of your household." The only thing I remember before fainting was the furrowed brow of the king as he yelled "Guards!"

Whew! *Finding the right words to express the right thoughts to get the right response is hard work.* And on top of that, it might not go as you planned or get the results that you wanted. Unfortunately, we can't anticipate what the outcome will be. However, this doesn't preclude the fact that planning is essential. But what's even more important is the ability to test the prevailing winds (receiver reactions) and adapt in the moment to ensure that the receiver gets what they deserve—I mean need. Let's return to the story of David and Bathsheba and look at Nathan's approach to this enormous feedback challenge.

Nathan told the king the story of the poor man who had nothing but a little lamb that he dearly loved. It was like a daughter to him. But a rich man took the poor man's lamb away. The rich man did not want "to take one of his own flock" to feed his guests.

Relating the parable of the rich man who took away the one little ewe lamb of his poor neighbor incited the king's anger against this unrighteous act. This story angered the king so much that he said to Nathan, "The man who has done this deserves to die. He shall restore the lamb fourfold, because he did this thing, and because he had no pity." Nathan's response to the king's distain for the rich man's act was direct. "It is you, King David, you are the man." David had become so insensitive to his sins that he didn't even realize that he was the villain in Nathan's story. The king at once confessed his sin and expressed sincere repentance.

For me, feedback is all about positioning (why something is being said), packaging (what is being said) and presentation (how it's being said). The key thoughts are that feedback is the story that you create (BS) as a result of your observations. Observation is watching something as it occurs, noting the things that stand out for you and later sharing your assessment of what you saw. Metaphorically, the BS in the form of feedback can be viewed as a gift. The positioning is your interpretation of what was observed. The packaging could be the wrapping paper that covers the gift—the message that you want to deliver as a result of your observations (e.g., the language you want to use, the intensity you want to project, etc.). The presentation is the delivery of the wrapped gift; exchanging information with the recipient: does the exchange involve leaving the gift at the front door, ringing the bell and running, forcing the gift into the mail slot (even if it doesn't fit?), or presenting the gift with flare and fanfare?

Giving feedback can sometimes be a challenging and uncomfortable venture. When giving feedback, there is an expectation that it will be received as intended and acted upon as expected. As the giver of feedback, "getting real" means you can't be either risk averse or emotionally insensitive. You have to be able to *delicately balance your intention to be supportive with the need to be truthful and the desire to be respectful.* Since respect is a subjective term, it's difficult to know where each person draws the "line" of respect. Though you certainly want to be aware of where that line is, you don't want to necessarily be limited by it. Adhering exclusively to someone else's line (or boundary) can dilute your message and potentially make it less meaningful. It's not as important that you be able to anticipate when the line has been crossed, as it is to be courageous enough to address it once it becomes obvious that it has. When the line is crossed, it's easy to lose focus, get frustrated, and run away. The boundary violation or the crossing the line can easily become the focus of the conversation—displacing the original focus, which was the feedback itself. This is a wonderful defense mechanism for those who aren't necessarily all that excited about the feedback to begin with.

If you're a receiver, to create value from the feedback you're given, you can't be too "thin-skinned," closed, or inflexible. Those who are able to get the most benefit from feedback are usually confident, not easily bruised, and most importantly, intellectually curious—capable of entertaining thoughts or perspectives that they don't necessarily agree with. Thinned-skinned, without a tough protective outer layer, it makes it much easier to get to delicate and sensitive internal organs, particularly the heart. Language is nuanced. Two people can hear the same thing and get totally difference meanings. These differences in hearing can in turn lead to differences in how people respond. This can, at times, be confusing and frustrating for both the giver and receiver.

The only way we can make sense out of the feedback we receive is to make connections between things, both environmental and experiential. When we measure new perceptions against prior world experiences, we're dealing in the world of expectations. Nathan had a long-standing relationship with King David. He understood that people often unknowingly condemn qualities in others that they don't see in themselves. Though there were many possible outcomes, Nathan's expectation was that his story would help King David measure his behaviors against his values to recognize the error of his ways and repent his sins. King David's expectation was that the culprit in Nathan's story would be duly punished. His expectations drove his choice of stories to tell to get the results he desired. Nathan had to make accurate judgments about future likelihoods. He had witnessed past outcomes that were less than desirable. Often if we revisit any given event, we realize that we had all the information we needed to make the appropriate decision prior to the event itself.

The intent of the preceding stories is to begin sensitizing us to biases that show up in our everyday experiences. BS is everywhere!

Section 3: Bias? What Bias?

❖ Biases
  ➤ All stories are susceptible to personal biases.
  ➤ We selectively choose data that supports what we already believe.
  ➤ We naturally rationalize, dispel or ignore any data that doesn't serve our interests.
  ➤ BS lives in the gap between "the truth" and our "personal truths."
  ➤ In the absence of evidence, we fill the gap with what we believe.

❖ Biased Stories
  ➤ The BS that we believe is often affected by our relationship with the BS'er.
  ➤ Making something "figural" means elevating and differentiating it from everything around it.
  ➤ Helping others to see something differently is creating new "awarenesses."
  ➤ Personal truths are stories that are so entrenched in our thinking that we no longer challenge their validity.

❖ Some common cognitive biases
  ➤ Confirmation bias—a preference for perspectives that reinforce or confirm what you already believe.
  ➤ Selection bias—a preference for facts that support your pre-existing beliefs.
  ➤ Expectancy bias—a preference for results that support your expected outcome
  ➤ Bandwagon bias—a preference for opinions that you feel will create the least conflict or division.
  ➤ Opportunity bias—a preference for a group that affords the preferred group unearned advantage.

IV. In Search of the Truth

Truth bears a greater burden of proof than mere facts, though facts form the underpinnings of truth. Objectivity allows relevant facts to guide rational thought in pursuit of truth. On the other hand, subjectivity allows preferred facts to guide biased thoughts that reinforce preexisting beliefs. When these two approaches to reality collide, the role of facts can be blurred.

A story is simply a narrative. It can take the form of either a novel or short story, fiction or nonfiction, prose or poetry. Regardless of the form it takes, all "good stories" have shared characteristics: they're clear, organized, and interesting and fulfill their intent. A "biased story" is one that is slanted in favor of some personal view. They can have a one-sided perspective that prevents the person having the bias from fully exploring the topic at hand. The bias becomes the dominant focus of the story. In fact, some biased stories are so "good" they can supersede or even subvert the truth. BS, no matter how unsubstantiated, is not "bad." It just "is." However, how we see and use our BS is the ultimate test of its value. BS can be used for "good"—to build, lift up, enable, and empower—or for "bad"—to tear down, divide, disable, and destroy. BS that supports exploration, research, and development could be considered the good application, and BS that is divisive or catalyzes war and dissent could be considered bad usage. However, once again, it's all BS.

Facts and Interpretation

As discussed previously, facts and interpretations play a significant role in not only understanding your own BS, but also understanding and appreciating the BS of others. Renee Loth of the *Boston*

Globe once wrote: "The ability to differentiate facts from interpretations has become a dying art… What's missing today is the discernment to tell the differences between fact and crap [which happens to be the name of a trivia board game]… The American people, it seems, have lost their BS detectors. Near universal access to information online has steadily devalued expertise and authority… Why insist on facts when everyone else is just 'speaking their own truth'?"

With the proliferation of stories that are misleading or false, and the depressing future projection of an exponential growth in fake stories, the ability to discern facts from interpretations is not only an important skill to have, but an absolute imperative in today's fast moving and ever-changing world of information. "Information overload" makes it hard for people to make decisions, even harder to know if the decisions you make are the right decisions, and harder still to stick with decisions once you've made them. Some information says yes. Some says no. What is true? What is right? Given the voluminous nature of data, how do we make choices?

You can find data that supports just about any choice that you make. But on the other hand, you can also find equally as much data to support any of a number of other choices or perspectives that are available to you. This creates a formidable dilemma when choosing anything—from a favorite political candidate to a special vacation destination to the best diapers for your baby. We're inundated with data continuously, from the time we wake up in the morning until the time we go to bed at night—from the places we frequent to the people we meet, to the television programs we watch—all are ever-present and ever-changing sources of new data.

So how do we make sense out of this continual barrage of data, data, and more data? My belief is that each of us has a built-in screening mechanism that is uniquely ours—something that gives us the power of discernment. Something that allows us to be slapped in the face daily with data from every direction, and then pick and choose only the data that is specifically tailored to serve our individual wants, needs, and curiosities. This magical screening device is none other than—*our values*, a special brand of BS.

I've heard values broadly described as the "secret sauce" that differentiates personal preferences in thoughts, actions, and outcomes—they are subjective, vary between individuals and cultures, and are reflective of our belief systems. They also have tremendous influence on our sense of what's right and wrong. (Note the use of qualifiers when describing values: "preference," "a person's," "subjective," "vary across individuals and cultures," "personal"—all intended to emphasize the fact that our values are uniquely ours.) Values form the filter through which all data flows and, correspondingly, the building block from which all BS emanates. All this is to, again, say that our BS is *uniquely ours*.

So returning to the original premise, it's easy to see how *we selectively choose data that either supports our beliefs or serves our interests.* There's obviously too much data for us to take it all in. So in any given situation, our built-in screening device kicks in, and certain parts of the environment just jump out at us. We don't even know how it happens—it just does. It's one of the magical gifts of creation that makes our lives interesting, ever changing, and distinctly unique.

Facts and interpretations are, figuratively speaking, the salt and pepper of story creation. They are the key to understanding why people have the stories they have and how those stories affect their views of the world. A phrase that might summarize the relationship "theory of different"—different facts and different interpretations result in different stories. So to be open, understanding, and accepting of those differences can lead us to a greater awareness of ourselves, others, and the world around us.

Facts are things that are accepted as being true. The phrase "accepted as being true" is a loaded phrase because some things that are accepted as being true aren't necessarily true (e.g., in America, everyone's vote counts equally). Statements that fall in the "possible but not certain" bucket are often called by some "debatable facts." Many believe that facts are indisputable and the key to objectivity. I believe that facts

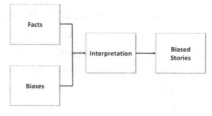

in and of themselves are completely objective, but the facts that we choose, the meaning that we infer, and the way we apply them are not. In other words, given the same set of facts, each person can and often does respond to them differently. Let's look at a simple example of a fact.

Fact: *James gave Diane a dozen roses.*

This statement is indisputable and easily verifiable. Right?

Biases are quite simply one-sided perspectives. They cause people to create their own "subjective reality," or unique view of the world. This reality isn't always based on facts, but to varying degrees can be influenced by facts depending on the openness of each person. As mentioned previously, there are a number of cognitive biases. These biases often skew logical thinking with personal preferences. Biased people generally believe what they want to believe rather than that which is factually true or agreeable to others. Biases can be based on differing thoughts, beliefs, or group affiliation where there is no neutral viewpoint.

Bias: *All people who give roses are romantics. James is a romantic because he gave Diane roses.* (Hasty generalization.)

Interpretations are the explanations for the things we experience. Facts, though considered to be indisputable, are nonetheless subject to interpretation. While an interpretation doesn't alter a fact, it does place it in a context that may either explain or change its significance. These interpretive explanations can take up permanent residency in our values, beliefs, assumptions, and understandings. In many cases we treat our interpretations as though they were facts! But interpretations are usually more intuitive than factual, and thereby bias by nature. They are the direct product of our creative mind. They are not necessarily void of reason, but quite often they are limited by reason.

Interpretation: *Roses are a symbol of love.*

That's one interpretation. A rose's symbolism varies according to its color and the number given. A red rose usually symbolizes love; a yellow rose, friendship; a pink rose, admiration; an orange rose, passion; a white rose, innocence. One rose symbolizes "infatuation," three "desire," six "love," nine "eternal love" (by the way—I wouldn't trust my explanation for the meaning of color or number).

Biased stories reflect how we apply our interpretations to real-world experiences. The facts we select and the interpretations we ascribe to those facts become our stories. Since we have complete discretion in which facts we choose and which interpretations we choose to explain them, the stories we create are inherently biased. So given the same set of facts, we may create completely different stories. You will notice that the further we move away from facts, the more subjective the statement becomes.

Story: *James gave Diane a dozen roses as an expression of his love.*

Again, this is one possible story. *"James gave Diane a dozen roses"* is indeed a fact. However, *"as an expression of his love"* is the story we created based on what we think is the reason for giving roses. The fact could be that James was driving Diane's new car when he sideswiped a parked car and had just returned from the auto body shop after receiving an exorbitant estimate for the cost of repair—none of which Diane had any knowledge of. The real reason why James was giving Diane a dozen roses was to provide a soft takeoff before a crash landing.

The "facts" we choose and the biases we have shape the "stories" we create. Contrary to popular belief, facts are neither good nor bad; they just "are." But choosing different facts can and often does lead to divergent perspectives. These divergent perspectives can at times escalate into irreconcilable differences or lead to previously unexplored paths of mutual discovery and reciprocal benefits. But for the latter to occur, those involved must be sincerely open, understanding, and accepting of differences. But as we may have experienced, most people aren't so accommodating.

Regardless of the *facts* that are available, people generally hear what they want to hear and believe what they want to believe. It's reasonable for a person to believe a story is false if there are few facts to support it or similarly believe a story is true if there are plenty of facts to support it. However, often times, people believe a story that is false despite there being plenty of factual support and true despite limited factual support.

Notice the perceived truthfulness of a story is directly correlated to a person's preexisting belief of its truthfulness regardless of the facts. As concluded in the University of Michigan study, when a misinformed person is exposed to true facts, they rarely change their minds. Therefore, in general, "feel" trumps "fact."

As stated previously, facts are things that are generally accepted as true. By definition, they are things that are "consistent with objective reality." They can be either tangible objects, sensory observations, or proven theories. In short, they are things that have been or can be verified through experimentation, observation, or measurement.

In today's cultural, spiritual, and political environment, the discernment of true facts from false assertions has become increasingly more difficult.

Let's begin the following discussion with a few myths about facts:

- Myth 1—*All facts are unbiased.*
  Facts are a partial sampling of reality, and we all view reality through different lenses. No one has the same perception even when viewing the same thing. You see "po-ta-to," I see "po-tat-o."
- Myth 2—*All beliefs that are supported by facts are true.*
  Even if valid facts are linked together, they can yield false results. The beliefs we have are a function of the *facts* we choose to accept as true.
- Myth 3—*The more facts you use to support an assertion, the truer the assertion is.*

We selectively choose facts to support what we already believe. So the number of facts used to support an assertion is less important than the "quality" and "relevance" of the facts chosen.

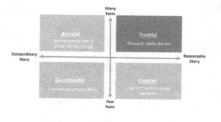

Facts are funny things. They invoke different responses in different people. For instance, I was at the gym with my nephew recently (not working out, just watching *Seinfeld* on the overhead TV monitor while waiting for my nephew to finish his workout). My nephew is a very athletically built young man with well-developed bis, tris, pecks, lats, hams, quads, calves, and a bunch of other long-neglected parts of my body. Although I do have a pretty pronounced and well-defined maximus abdominus (big gut, for short). That's enough about me. Back to my nephew. Someone at the gym had obviously been watching my nephew as he went through his customary rigorous workout regimen. The onlooker took advantage of an infrequent break in my nephew's routine to casually strike up a conversation.

He asked, "What kind of routine do you use—circuit training, isometrics, push-pull…You look pretty solid. How much do you weigh?"

My nephew politely responded, "Hundred and eighty pounds."

He continued, "How tall are you?"

My nephew said, "Six feet."

Having listened to this exchange standing only a few feet away, I decided to join in. I walked over to the two of them and injected my unsolicited observation.

I shared, "I hadn't realized it, but my nephew and I are the same height and weight." I added humorously, "We're almost like twins," as I playfully flashed my version of a bicep flex.

What came next was one of the most deflating responses I'd ever received.

The person who had been querying my nephew turned to me and said, "Don't delude yourself. You're just a skinny bag of bones with an oversize head. Whereas, he [referring to my nephew] has perfect proportions and incredible muscular definition. He looks really good."

Let's just focus on that "skinny" thing for a minute. Aside from me being extremely hurt by his harsh (but perhaps "true") assessment of my physique (which I like to consider a work in progress), that "skinny" thing stood out for me. How could my nephew and I have the same dimensions (height and weight), yet I'm skinny and he's proportionate. That's when it once again dawned on me—it's all BS.

In another life, I once conducted corporate workshops on communications. We had one activity that we used to discern "facts and interpretations." In this exercise, the participants would first be provided with a list of random words describing physical attributes, like *fat, skinny, tall, short*, etc. Then we would move on to other words that referenced social attributes, like *friendly, successful, kind, happy, generous*, etc. Then we would move on to more socially and politically provocative words, like *fair, just, equitable*, etc. The question posed to the audience for each word was "Is this word fact or interpretation?"

The responses were very revealing. As noted previously, many characterized the physical attributes as "facts" (some more vehemently than others). When asked to describe what was "fat" or "skinny," for example (not wanting to offend anyone in the room), they usually used the name of a well-known celebrity (imagery). And depending on the celebrity chosen, they would either get affirmation or disapproval from others in the group. When pressed further as to why they felt that particular celebrity was "fat/skinny," they would usually fumble around (still not wanting to offend) until the *"pundit-types"* landed on "It's obvious—look at him," or the *"scientific-types"* landed on the specific height and weight that they felt would qualify a person as being "fat/skinny" (different, of course, for men versus women).

So we asked the group, "How many believe that celebrity X is fat/skinny?" Depending on the celebrity, the responses would often vary along the continuum from "strongly agree" to "strongly disagree." We would then have someone look up statistics on the physical stature of the chosen celebrity (or defer to a knowledgeable member of the audience) and find exactly how tall celebrity X was and how much they weighed (in other words, do a little "research"). We then posed the question "How many agree that celebrity X is xx inches tall and weighs xx lbs?" There would usually be almost unanimous agreement. We would then ask the question "Is 'fat' a fact or interpretation?" At this point, there would be almost unanimous agreement that "fat" is indeed an interpretation! (Trumpets would sound, confetti would drop from the ceiling, everyone would hold hands singing "kum ba yah" and chanting "fat and skinny are dead—it's height and weight instead—lala lala lala.)

In the midst of our celebration of this new awareness, there would always be one voice (usually coming from somewhere in the back of the room) that would say, "CELEBRITY X IS STILL FAT!" What? Oh no, they didn't! But regretfully, yes, they did. How would you respond to this obvious "awareness-deficient interpretation dissident" (I don't really know what that means, but it does sound like a pretty good "dis." Do they use "dis" for "disparate" anymore? They never did? Oh, anyway, I digress).

Some possible responses might be, "You couldn't be more wrong. Fat is an interpretation. We just 'proved' it," or "This is the sensitive aware group, not the ADID group [short for awareness-deficient interpretation disorder]. You need to find your own group." Herein lies the challenge of discerning facts from interpretations. In many cases, our interpretations *are* our facts! Interpretations are more intuitive than factual. They are the direct product of our creative mind or our imagination. Interpretations are not necessarily *void* of reason, but quite often, they are limited by reason. Interpretations are born out of personal beliefs rather than empirical facts, and thereby bias by nature.

Though many would beg to differ, "skinny" is not a fact (nor am I "skinny"; I consider myself "pleasingly slight"). These descriptions are merely perceptions based on "sensory" observations. We see something, and it creates an immediate impression. We describe our impression using language that is more "soft" than "substantive," more subjective than factual. So it doesn't matter what the guy at the gym said about me or what the person in the back of the room said about the celebrity. It doesn't matter whether a person is seen as quiet, attractive, and articulate or gregarious, imposing, and assertive. It's all BS! (My story and I'm sticking to it.)

The stories we create about people, places, experiences, and life have basically two components: facts and beliefs. Facts are the parts of the story that are objective, logical, and quantifiable (e.g., nonfiction). Beliefs are those parts that are subjective, intuitive, imaginative, and biased (e.g., fiction).

Facts are logic-based truths. They are considered rational, coherent, reasoned, and consistent with other related facts. They are considered accurate based on what we know today. Consequently, they usually represent the end of scientific inquiry. However, that doesn't mean that facts are always true. They are considered "true" until new information is introduced that challenges their credibility and catalyzes the need for further inquiry. By way of example, many believed the earth was flat until about the sixth century BC. We may find that humorous today, but people didn't have evidence that the earth was spherical until about 330 BC (Aristotle). That's a huge swath of time, from the sixth to the fourth century, which the flat-earth theory was considered to be a fact. I'm sure initial discussions of the earth being spherical were thought to be heretical. Today we have satellites everywhere that provide sophisticated real-time images of the earth. Yet and still there are groups today that continue to claim that the earth is flat. (And just in case you're wondering, no, I'm not a member. I'm a member of the "Corporations Are People Club.")

Beliefs are often confused with facts and thought to be true. However, "a belief is only true if it corresponds to a fact and is part of a coherent system of beliefs." It would be inconsistent to say "all immigrants are disloyal to America. John is an immigrant, but John isn't disloyal to America." This statement begins with a belief—"all immigrants are disloyal to America." Is this belief true or false? Hm, I think I'll go with false, Alex, since I haven't seen a study that includes "all" immigrants. If I had said I haven't seen a study that says "all immigrants are disloyal to America," a true-blue believer might respond, "You haven't seen a study that says they aren't all disloyal either, now, have you?" and I would have to agree. This would put me on the defensive. Then I would have to say, "But I haven't seen a study that includes all immigrants." Unfortunately, the moment would be lost. My affirmative response to the believer's first question would have been all that s/he needed to declare victory.

This is a very clever rhetorical trick akin to "bait and switch." When you ask for proof that something is true, the person you're talking to, in turn, asks you to provide proof that it isn't. Try it. It works. Just make some off-the-wall assertion, like, "I think the sky is falling." A probable response is, "That's ridiculous! What evidence do you have that the sky is falling?" You respond, "What evidence do you have that it isn't?" Bam! Game over! You win!

Now, as I was saying, "All immigrants are disloyal. John is an immigrant, and John isn't disloyal" offers an incoherent system of beliefs. So by definition, it can't be true. For one, John being loyal is inconsistent with "all" being disloyal. I know the intent was to say that John is the exception. However, this admission leaves open the possibility that other exceptions may exist.

But it really doesn't matter whether the belief is part of a coherent system of beliefs or is disputed by an overabundance of facts. It only mattered that the person who said it believes it to be true. This is a case of blind BS, holding on to a belief unconditionally despite evidence to the contrary—even evidence that you are aware of and personally believe! Logic often ends where bias begins.

One of the fundamental skills for effectively wading through all the BS we get hit with daily is the ability to *discern "true" facts from fake "facts."* Fake facts may initially appear to be an oxymoron. True facts are those that have been systematically proven to be true. Fake facts are those that are unproven but often accepted as true. The following list, which is adapted from an Auburn University whitepaper, offers some distinctions between true and false facts.

"True" Facts

- **Empirical Facts:** Empirical facts are the results of *convergent scientific observations*. Scientific observations begin as simple suppositions that seem to be reasonably valid but have limited evidential support (e.g. "The earth is flat"). They begin as hypotheses that are proven or disproven through systematic testing (e.g., "The earth is spherical."). Those that are proven true are accepted as empirical fact. Empirical facts must withstand all subsequent scientific challenges to their validity (e.g., "The earth is cubical... Nope, still spherical"). If the empirical facts remain intact despite all challenge, they are considered to be facts that have been validated through a convergence of all scientific observations.

- **Analytical Facts**: Analytic facts are verified through *logical reasoning*. These facts begin with a problem to be solved. They then use a systematic process of breaking the problem down into smaller parts to solve it. Analysis involves reviewing data and identifying trends to solve problems (e.g., like Sherlock Holmes using deductive reasoning to solve his cases). It's more "formulaic" than quantitative. For example, if John is the same age as Sue and Sue is the same age as Ralph, then John is the same age as Ralph. This logic holds true regardless of the ages of John, Sue and Ralph. The reason why they are facts is because they have survived the rigors of logical testing and work in all circumstances. However, beware of false logic. Some might say if the previous example is true, then if John lives next door to Sue, and Sue lives next door to Ralph, then John must live next door to Ralph. This example is not always true so would not be considered an analytic fact.

- **Evaluative Facts:** Evaluative facts are verified by applying *objective standards* of value. Let's use the edict "Thou shall not speed" to explain evaluative facts. The objective standard for speeding is obviously the posted speed limit. The police use their radar guns to capture a car's actual speed. So the evaluative fact, the car was speeding, is verified by comparing the speed of the car against the posted speed limit. This leads to the conclusion (evaluative fact) that the car was either speeding or not. When subjective standards are used, certain evaluative facts can be confused with opinions. By way of example, I'm sure many of us have either said or heard someone say, "That person is really a poor leader." The objective standard could be something as simple as how many times they cancelled a staff meeting. This may be an objective standard, but not one that is shared by others.

Fake "Facts"

- **"Alternative Facts"**: (Intuitive facts) Alternative facts are untested assertions that may have some evidence to support them, but the evidence is not convergent or supported by other related observations (e.g., "There is massive voter fraud."). Untested claims may be too vague, ambiguous, or incomplete to determine their validity. These claims often fall in the realm of opinions, particularly when they are untested "evaluative" claims (e.g., "Lebron is the best basketball player in history."). This assertion leaves unanswered "By what standards?" So this assertion may or may not be true depending on the standards used to validate the assertion. Alternative facts can also be those chosen to rationalize or justify rather than validate or substantiate a chosen position.

- **False "Facts":** How can a fact be false? It's a commonly used psychological game. It's like saying if you can't "prove" me wrong, then I must be right (e.g., "The world is coming to an end on December 21st." ... and after December 21st ... "Oh, you misunderstood. I meant December 21st 2099."). False facts are claims that are contradicted by all available relevant evidence. Though unsubstantiated, they are still presented as though they were fact. These claims can be knowingly false or erroneously believed to be true. The claim that the earth is flat is a false factual claim. Yet it was once believed to be true. Using the claim that "drinking 2–3 glasses of wine a day improves heart health" to justify drinking 6 glasses a day is obviously false logic. (After all, if 3 is good, then 6 must be twice as good. It's only logical.)

- **Belief-Based "Facts":** Beliefs are obviously not the same as facts. Although facts can be integral to beliefs. Some beliefs are based on thoroughly researched and validated theory or thought. While others are based on pure conjecture. It's similar to the chicken and egg dilemma, "which came first?" Were the facts chosen to support the belief or was the belief developed based on the facts. If it's the former it's what I call a belief-based "fact" or a belief masquerading as a fact. For instance, "the earth is flat," "the sun revolves around the earth" and "climate change is a hoax" are beliefs that defy proven facts. "Democrats are compassionate," "Republicans are patriotic" and "Independents are discerning" are gen-

eralizations that are not necessarily substanti-
ated by unbiased facts.

Facts are usually thought to be statements that have been proven
by scientific observation. Since most of us are not scientist and don't
know the first thing about scientific methods, facts can simply be
defined as things that can be shown to be true and are also supported
by a "convergence of evidence." That "convergent evidence" thing
is extremely important. We all know that evidence can be real or
made up. The word *convergent* is derived from the Latin *convergere*
and simply means "coming together." So convergent evidence just
means that all relevant evidence comes together to support any given
perspective.

When we experience something, we form an immediate
impression that we express using descriptive language. These initial
responses are often void if corroborating facts. The sensations vary
from person to person, as do the stories that are created. With differing and often divergent "stories," facts should be the anchor on
which the credibility of a story is determined. Without facts, stories
are just fanciful creations.

I'm sure we can all think of examples of people who have made
statements that they claim to be true, and after examining the facts,
it becomes quite evident that their statements are the farthest thing
from the truth. Yet despite an overwhelming amount of data to the
contrary, they still hold on to the truth of their perspective. They
selectively choose only the facts, no matter how limited, that they feel
support their perspective. So facts are excluded at the discretion of the
person telling the story. Similarly, they may be excluded at the discretion of the listener. But that doesn't mean that the excluded facts
are not relevant. Indeed, many facts that are ignored are extremely
relevant and, in many cases, *the most relevant*. It's just that they either
don't fit into the speaker's (or listener's) sensibilities or serve their
purpose.

The other day I was listening to a political pundit respond to a
question about her stance on the pressing issue of the day. She began
by presenting an exhaustive (and rather impressive) list of "fake facts"

to support her position. She spouted these fake facts with such fervor and flare that had I not been able to do some basic research on the issue, I might have begun to question my own position, which was the polar opposite of the position she was taking. She was actually very good (at manipulating fake facts to support her position). She seemed to believe that inundating her audience with large volumes of seemingly credible information was enough to convince them of the rightness of her position. And for many, this worked. But even though I'm not always successful, I try to *never let form supersede substance or volume obscure quality*. There is absolutely no correlation between the style of the presenter, the volume of information they offer, and the validity of their story. If there were, it would simplify things considerably. We could just pay attention to whoever sounded the most convincing or presented the most "facts" on either side of any given story to determine which side was valid. Unfortunately, it's not that easy. Facts are often elusive. There are many types of both real and pseudo facts that can be used to muddy the waters. So it's extremely important that essential facts be differentiated from subjective interpretations. Not only do we view "facts" differently, we select different "facts."

Truth versus Credible BS

When do our stories become normalized? By normalized, I mean become a standard part of our broader belief system? It is usually when they cross the threshold that we use to demark "the truth." Thoughts, feelings, opinions, beliefs, and judgments that are created in our heads, though subjective, are often considered to be true. Things that are commonly accepted as measurable, observable, unbiased, and factual, though objective, can be seen as untrue. How is that even possible? So objectivity and subjectivity are not always the baseline for personal truth. The single most important determinant of a person's truth is "belief." As stated previously, if we believe something to be true, we find ways to rationalize it. And if we believe it to be untrue, we seek to find ways to mitigate or deny it. This thing that we will defend to the end regardless of the facts I call "credible BS."

"Credible BS" rules the world. It's prevalent in every aspect of our private and social lives. Credibility is more a function of trust than truth. Trust is highly subjective. It can allow a gap to comfortably exist between what we choose to believe and what is factually true. It can cause us to accept without question positions that are otherwise untenable. One well-known politician once boasted, "I could stand in the middle of Fifth Avenue and shoot somebody and I wouldn't lose voters." This is an example of loyalty and trust that is independent of facts or reality. In this case, faith in the messenger is sufficient validation of the message.

Please don't get credible BS confused with "truth," as many often do. Credible BS just means that you are able to convince a lot of people (who probably already agree with you) that your thoughts, feelings, and beliefs, no matter how unsubstantiated, are valid. Credible BS is much more pervasive and impactful in our daily lives than the truth. "Why?" you might ask. Because as Jack Nicholson so forcefully stated in the movie *A Few Good Men*—"You can't handle the truth!" To seek truth requires discipline, openness, discernment, and humility. And even with due diligence and hard work, the results of truth-seekers are usually nebulous at best. Credible BS is often more readily available and easily digested than the truth. It requires little or no effort to claim something is true. Whereas it requires substantially more effort to prove something true.

Truth is verifiable and undeniable—independent of how it affects or is received by others. Truth is grounded in reality and based on indisputable facts (if there are such things). So to stand on truth is often to stand in direct opposition to what people see as true, or "credible BS." It is at times extremely difficult to discern the difference between truth and "credible BS."

Though truth is elusive, facts are less so. Facts can provide a foundation on which both truth and credible BS can be built. You would think that the more facts there are, the more credible the BS should be. Unfortunately, this is not necessarily so. It turns out that the stronger your belief, regardless of the facts, the more credible the BS is perceived to be.

As discussed previously, identifying the truth is, at times, a slippery slope. So often the "truths" we tell ourselves are merely fragments of the truth (personal truths), and sometimes they're not really truth at all. In any situation there can be any number of facts and equally as many interpretations.

Thoughts, feelings, opinions, beliefs, and judgments that are created in our own heads are by definition subjective. Things that are commonly accepted as factual, measurable, and unbiased (real, rational, reliable, and relevant) are generally seen as true. It is certainly possible to meld the two together and have thoughts, feelings, and opinions that are factual and unbiased.

A former mayor of New York City once famously said "Truth isn't truth" when defending his decision to counsel his well-known client not to testify in front of a US Special Counsel. In the lead up to this absurd statement, he said, "And when you tell me that...he 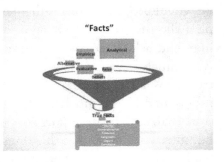 should testify because he's going to tell the truth and he shouldn't worry, well, that's silly because it's somebody's version of the truth. Not the truth..."

The interviewer responded, "Truth is truth..."

The former mayor responded in turn, "No, it isn't truth. TRUTH ISN'T TRUTH!"

I think what the mayor was trying to say is that we all have beliefs or "personal truths" that can be quite different from one another. If one person's "personal truth" differs from another's, which is "THE TRUTH"? (Note: This is a rehash of the small "t," capital "T" distinction presented earlier.)

This has never been a dilemma for me. The story that is supported by the overwhelming preponderance of convergent facts is the one that rings true for me (Note I didn't say it is true). The facts I'm referring to are not just any facts, but *facts that are real, rational, reliable,* and *relevant.* "Real" means facts that are not false, imagined, or contrived. "Rational" means facts that are logically connected to one another and part of a larger coherent system of facts. "Reliable" means facts that are consistently dependable. "Relevant" means facts that are appropriate to what is being considered.

We use our internal filters to differentiate between "true facts" and "fake facts." The identification of "true facts" has become increasingly more difficult. If we are indeed able to discern "true facts" from those that are fake, then it automatically follows that if we use those "true facts" we will create a "true" narrative. We will have arrived at "the truth." Right? Not quite. As seen in the previous discussion on voter fraud, "true facts" can yield "false conclusions." For example, everyone knows that if A=B and B=C, then A=C. So it logically follows that if John lives next to Sally (fact) and Sally lives next to Ron (fact), then John lives next to Ron, Right? No, wrong! So a word of caution, once the true facts have been identified, caution must be taken to ensure that the final narrative combines these facts in a way that is comprehensive, coherent, and convergent.

- *Comprehensive* means taking all "true" facts into consideration.
- *Coherent* means use of facts is reasoned and consistent.
- *Convergent* means all facts taken together create an unquestionably decisive conclusion.

Facts don't necessarily have the power to change minds, though they can. But more often than not, they do just the opposite. In a series of studies in 2005 and 2006, researchers at the University of Michigan found that when misinformed people, particularly political partisans, were exposed to corrected facts in news stories, they rarely changed their minds. In fact, they often became even more strongly set in their beliefs. Facts, they found, were not curing misinformation. Like an underpowered antibiotic, facts could actually make misinformation even stronger.

As stated previously, true stories are usually validated by an overwhelming *convergence of facts*. Essential facts should all come together in support of a valid assertion. During the iconic O. J. Simpson trial, the late Johnnie Cochran famously said, "If the glove doesn't fit, you must acquit." I think what Mr. Cochran was saying (using bad rhyme) was that if this one fact wasn't true (the glove fitting), the current charges against OJ should be dropped. Or in the same vein, "If the facts don't fit, the story is illegit." (Johnny Cochran isn't the only one with rhymes.)

To determine if "the facts fit and the story is legit, the following questions may help:

- Comprehensive: *What are all the relevant facts (investigation)?* The systematic examination of the narrative.
- Coherent: *What facts are used to support the prevailing story (corroboration)?* Confirmation of the findings.
- Convergent: *What story would all facts taken together support (consolidation)?* Combining relevant facts into a coherent whole.

These questions are not only intended to help differentiate between the facts and interpretations of a story, but also highlight the biases in our selection of facts used to either support or refute a story.

The question that is most elusive in the real world is convergence. As we've discussed, the leap from fact to story is almost automatic. We see something happen and we create a story to explain it. However, the validation and reconciliation of differing stories is where the challenge comes in. As a matter of fact, reconciling differing stories is so difficult that many avoid it altogether. The reason it is so hard is because it requires a person to suspend their perspective (not give it up, just suspend it) so they can see other perspectives. Why? Because sometimes it's difficult to see multiple perspectives clearly at the same time.

Convergence is necessary for understanding and reconciliation. Reconciliation is the act of restoring something to its normalized state. An example of a formalized convergence process was the work of The Truth and Reconciliation Commission (TRC) of South Africa. The TRC was a court-like body assembled by Archbishop Desmond Tutu after the end of Apartheid. Anybody who felt they had been a victim of violence could come forward and be heard at the TRC. Perpetrators of violence could also give testimony and request amnesty from prosecution. The formal hearings began on April 15, 1996. The hearings made international news and many sessions were broadcast on national television. The TRC was a crucial component of the transition to full and free democracy in South Africa and, despite some flaws, is generally regarded as having been very successful. The TRC was a part of the Promotion of National Unity and Reconciliation Act of 1995 based in Cape Town. The mandate of the commission was to bear witness to, record and in some cases grant amnesty to the perpetrators of crimes relating to human rights violations, reparation and rehabilitation." (SAHO South African History Online—The Truth and Reconciliation Commission)

So convergence and reconciliation in combination are essentially about being presented with all the facts and given the opportunity to reconcile differences. Convergence ensures that all the facts continue to support your story and, if not, using the new understanding of relevant facts to create a new story.

Real World Example

Many of you might be familiar with the following example which has been covered extensively in the media. I chose this example because it's illustrative, contemporary, and polarizing. Yep, you heard right. I wanted something that was controversial. Why do I like controversial topics? I choose these topics "not because they are easy, but because they are hard; because that goal will serve to organize and measure the best of our energies and skills, because that challenge is one that we are [I am] willing to accept." (John F. Kennedy, Moon Speech—Rice Stadium, September 12, 1962). Not really. The real reason is that it was the first thing that came to mind as I was writing.

One well-known story that created mayhem in a past national election was the claim that millions of people voted illegally. Let's revisit this story using the previously offered three-question scheme: What are the relevant facts? Which facts are used to support the story? and What story would all facts support?

Comprehensive: *What are all the relevant facts?*

Some of the relevant facts presented were from the Pew Charitable Trusts Report. They were as follows:

- There are millions of voter registration inaccuracies.
- 2.75 million people were registered to vote in two states.
- 1.8 million dead people are on the voter rolls.
  (FactCheck.Org: Deception on Voter Fraud; January 26, 2017 and *Los Angeles Times* article on the Pew Center study on voter fraud by Kurtis Lee)

The results of an ongoing examination of voter fraud claims by the Brennan Center for Justice revealed the following:

- Incident rates for voter fraud were between .0003 percent and .0025 percent.
- Voter fraud is very rare.
- Voter impersonation is nearly non-existent (higher probability of being struck by lightning).
- No evidence of people voting in multiple states.
  (Brennan Center for Justice—at New York University School of Law: Debunking the Voter Fraud Myth—January 25, 2017)

Discovery Evidence: a study conducted by David Becker, the director of the Center for Election Innovation and Research, found these:

- No evidence of voter fraud, let alone millions of illegal ballots.
- No evidence that any fraudulent votes were cast.
- 1.8 million dead people were still listed as voters, but there was no evidence that anyone had voted in their names.
- 2.75 million people were registered to vote in multiple states, which is not illegal (unless they voted in multiple states).

Coherent: *What facts are used to support the prevailing stories?*

- Story A: *"Millions of people voted illegally in the last election."*
  - o 1.8 million dead people on the voter rolls
  - o 2.75 million people registered to vote in multiple states

- Story B: *"There is no evidence of widespread voter fraud."*
  - o Voter impersonation is nearly nonexistent
  - o No evidence of people voting in multiple states

Convergence: *What story is supported by all the facts?*
Convergent Evidence:

- The incident rate for voter fraud is between .0003% and .0025%.
- There are 1.8 million dead people on the voting rolls. There is no evidence that any dead people actually voted.
- There are 2.75 million people registered to vote in two states. There is no evidence that anyone voted in two states.

This illustrates why convergent evidence is so important. *Each fact taken alone can paint quite a different picture than all facts taken together.* It is very easy to leap from 1.8 million dead people on the voting rolls or 2.75 million people registered in two states, which are facts, to "voter fraud." However, if we think about it, that's a giant leap that leaves a lot of questions unanswered. How did that many dead people get on the voter rolls? Has anyone assumed the identity of those people? If yes, how many? Did they vote using the stolen identity? Did they vote multiple times using their identity and the stolen identity? But rather than pursue the answers to these questions through legitimate investigative research, it is easier to selectively use only the facts that support what we already believe. This is allowing the belief to drive our choice of facts rather than facts driving what we believe.

In order to make the leap from "1.8 million dead people on the voting rolls" to "voter fraud," one would have to assume that the dead people were left on or illegally added to the rolls for nefarious reasons. You would also have to assume that votes were cast in the name of a significant number of them. Now that would indeed be voter fraud. But to get there, all the interim assumptions would have to be true: (1) the 1.8 million names on the voting rolls were there illegally and (2) votes were actually cast using those names.

We know that in the absence of facts, assumptions fill the gap. Assumptions are not facts. They are merely personal beliefs that reflect our biases. We believe them to be true with or without proof. If we believe 1.8 million dead people are registered to vote "illegally," then there must be something "wrong." ("After all, they're dead. How could that be legal?") And if we believe that people are illegally voting using the assumed names of dead people, and we find one (a single) example of this actually happening, we can and often do use this single incident to justify our conspiratorial belief that the same thing is happening for all the dead people. "Isn't it logical to assume that if it happened once, it could have happened 1.8 million times?" Well, no. One out of 1.8 million is .000056 percent. The odds of being killed by an elephant falling from a coconut tree in downtown Los Angeles are probably higher. But why let the facts get in the way of a perfectly good story? It happened once, then it could have happened a thousand or even 1.8 million times. Believe it!

It's very interesting how facts were used to both create and, subsequently, justify the validity of the "voter fraud" story. In creating the story, facts were used to appeal both logically and emotionally to the listener. It's not unreasonable for there to be an emotional reaction to the fact that there were 1.8 million dead people on voter rolls. "Dead people don't vote. Why are they registered? That can't be right. There must be something shady going on here." Given this fact alone, that's certainly not an unreasonable story to create. Nor is it unreasonable to think "Hmmmm, people die all the time. I'm sure states don't regularly scrub their voter rolls to remove the names of those who have died. So having a significant number of deceased on the voting rolls is certainly understandable."

Given a single fact without further evidence or explanation, most people have an immediate visceral response. It's either "right" or "wrong." In this example, there is an emotional appeal to our collective sense of morality. The thought of someone "being registered to vote in multiple states"—can't be right, can it?—leading to the conclusion (that has got to be wrong). What if after further investigation, we find this is not abnormal. Families often don't go through the process necessary to get loved ones off the rolls because of oversight or it's just not a priority. Now on top of that, let me add that these dead people are voting (outrage). And the icing on the cake, we have real, factual data that this is occurring (demonstrations in the streets).

However, at this point, both stories are simply BS. Both draw conclusions with a very limited number of facts—one, to be exact. And as I shared previously, in the absence of facts, assumptions fill the gap. The first perspective assumed that the dead people were on the rolls "illegally." The second assumed that there was a "legitimate reason" for dead people appearing on the rolls. At this point, neither of these assumptions has been proven true. So the same fact gave rise to two completely divergent perspectives.

There was one more assertion that was presented as fact. That was the assertion that these dead people actually voted! On the surface, it might seem as though this assertion could be easily verified or dispelled. Not necessarily. Since 1.8 million people have already been identified, from a statistical standpoint, it would seem to be a fairly easy task to go back and find out how many of them voted. You would think. But maybe not.

Assume that the results of your investigation showed fifty (50) of the 1.8 million dead people actually cast votes. This would definitely be enough to prove that there was indeed voter fraud. But maybe not enough to make exaggerated claims of "widespread systematic" voter fraud. (Note that 50 represents .00278% of 1.8 million.) Is this statistically significant? You be the judge. The "widespread systematic" part is pure hyperbole meant to up the emotional response.

Assume that the results showed that none (zero) of the registered dead people actually voted. That should be a slam dunk, right? Everyone would then agree that there was no voter fraud, right?

Wrong! From the Michigan study we know that once we believe something to be true, we find ways to justify our belief despite overwhelming evidence to the contrary—"The investigation was flawed," "The investigator was biased," "The sampling inadequate." This is not unusual, nor is it unique to this issue. *We all create our own stories based on what we know, what we think we know, what we perceive to be true, or what we want others to believe is true.*

Section 4: In Search of the Truth

- ❖ A fundamental skill for wading through BS is the ability to *discern facts from interpretations.*
- ❖ Facts are logic based truths and represent the end of scientific inquiry. These are the different types of "facts":
    - ➤ *Empirical facts* are the results of convergent scientific observations systematic testing.
    - ➤ *Analytic facts* begin with a problem to be solved and are resolved through logical reasoning.
    - ➤ *Evaluative* facts are verified by applying objective standards to determine validity.
    - ➤ *Intuitive facts*, also referred to as "alternative facts," are untested assertions that may have some evidence to support them, but the evidence is not supported by other related observations.
    - ➤ *False facts* are claims that are contradicted by all available relevant evidence but presented as though they were true.
- ❖ "Credible BS" is a story that is believable independent of substantiating evidence
    - ➤ Arguably more pervasive and impactful in our daily lives than the truth.
    - ➤ Often more readily available and easily digested than the truth.

86

Often more a function of trust than truth

❖ Truth is verifiable and undeniable
  ➤ Truth is grounded in reality and based on indisputable facts (if there are such things).
  ➤ To stand on truth is often to stand in direct opposition to credible BS.
  ➤ Though truth is elusive, facts are less so.
  ➤ Facts can provide a foundation for both the truth and credible BS.
❖ Considerations for validating facts
  ➤ Identify 'hard' facts and 'soft' interpretations.
  ➤ Determine if the facts presented are from a reputable source (i.e., websites).
  ➤ For any survey, check a sample choice and size to ensure it is statistically significant.
  ➤ For any opinion piece ensure that the facts used are credible and the conclusion logical.
  ➤ Consider the motivation of the author (i.e. inform, instruct, influence etc.).
  ➤ Be sensitive to the nature of the story; is it singularly biased or well rounded.
❖ Story Creation
  ➤ Reasoning is often used to justify rather than validate a story.
  ➤ Stories are generally simplified and selective reconstructions of things from our past (McAdams).
  ➤ Stories are often based on what we think we know, what we perceive to be true or what we want others to believe.
  ➤ We create stories organically from "sensations" (e.g. experience, an observation, a conversation, etc.).
  ➤ Stories are a product of both reality (facts) and imagination (interpretations).
  ➤ Divergent stories can be created from the same facts.

> ➤ Convergent evidence provides greater insights into divergent stories.
- ❖ Questions that can help validate a story
  - ➤ What are all the available facts?
  - ➤ What are the relevant facts?
  - ➤ What facts support the story?
  - ➤ What other stories do the facts support?
  - ➤ What is the most reasonable story based on the facts?

V. The Tale the Teller Told

BS comes in a variety of colors. Just as mixing different combinations of basic colors can produce an expanded palette of new colors, selective combinations of facts, sprinkled with a little imagination, can likewise be used to generate an expanded palette of new stories.

Types of BS

In observing the current presidential race, it is not unusual to hear one candidate accuse another of being a "liar." Whereas this was once considered taboo, it appears to now be rather common. But the word *lie* is obviously a loaded word regardless of the context in which it is used. However, the way we frame the word gives us an indication of just how much bias played in our decision to call someone a liar. There are several ways this might be approached.

1.   One way may be to say *"The facts don't support what you said." (And I've done my homework.)*

This kind of a systematic approach where "facts" are central to the decision is often more acceptable depending on the choice of facts.

2.   Another may be to say *"In my experience that hasn't been true." (And believe me, I have a lot of experience.)*

Implicit in this statement is that the person speaking has some experiential knowledge of the subject being discussed.

3. A third may be to say *"That is probably not true."* *(And from my perspective, it doesn't make logical sense.)*

This person qualifies their position by using the word *probably*, giving it a tone of uncertainty; it could be true, but it's probably not.

4. Another may be to say *"That was a lie."* *(At least that's what I want you to believe.)*

This position sounds firm, conclusive, and resolute but is more often than not self-serving, insincere, and hypocritical.

5. And a final one may be to say *"That was a lie!"* *(And that's what I really believe.)*

This position is emphatic, unequivocal, absolute, and totally sincere!

But which approach is better? The answer is, it depends. (I'm sure you've never heard that before.) But it really does depend on your BS "proclivities." (What kind of philosophical BS is that?) To identify your particular proclivities, I've developed something I call the *BS index.* It is intended to offer distinctions for different types of BS'ers. No one is purely a single type in all circumstances. Our storytelling tendencies are generally an amalgamation of all types. You'll note that there are some clear distinctions in the language that differentiates each approach from the others. The distinctions are closely related to the way data is used in each approach. Let's give a name to each of the aforementioned approaches. *This acknowledges the nuance in differing perspectives.*

1. The first will be subsequently referred to as the "scientist." Scientists generally form a hypothesis and use relevant data to test the validity of that hypothesis. It's important to emphasize that true scientists try to take into consideration all data—that which seemingly supports their hypothesis and that which may contradict it. If the test reveals an over-

whelming amount of data that contradicts the hypothesis, then the scientists may conclude that "the facts don't support" their original assertion so it is therefore false. The problem comes when the research method is flawed. (*My research has proven this to be untrue.*) Testing has proven that the antioxidants in red wine increases high-density lipoprotein (HDL) cholesterol, offering some protection against arterial blood vessels. (Measurable characteristics of the data; hypothesis, key factors, and data selection.)

2. Expert (*my assessment has determined this to be untrue*)— red wine in moderation helps protect against obesity and diabetes / reduces risk of inflammation and blood clotting. (Selective awareness of data.)

3. Pundit (*my experience causes me to believe this is untrue*)— the glass contains red wine made from the finest grapes. (Assertions drawn from the data.)

4. Opportunist (*I choose to accept that is untrue*)—if advantageous, can rationalize taking both sides of any contested issues. A representative for a vineyard may say red wine has more heart heathy benefits than all other types of alcoholic beverages. (A purposeful—self-serving—application of data.)

BS Index

5. Idealist (*I believe this to be unquestionably untrue*)—the alcoholic content of wine makes it unhealthy. (Rationalization in place of data)/idealists don't equivocate or deal in nuance.

Scientist

"Where do you want to go on vacation?" my wife asked.

"I want to go any place where there's sun, sand, and surf" was my response. Simple, direct, and to the point.

However, a scientific BS-er may respond to the same question with a little different flavor. Their response may sound something like this: "We should firstly be concerned about the risk factors for sunburn, because sunburn can contribute to possible skin irritation, skin damage, and even skin cancer, depending on the amount of exposure to UV rays. My age, fair skin, and moles and your freckles, antibiotics, and acne make our skin more sensitive to the sun and increase the risk of possible skin damage. We probably want to go someplace with lots of sun but cooler air temperatures. The Canary Islands would be a good choice because they are near the sea where the trade winds blow mostly from the northeast and keep the heat from building up during the day. Also, most of the time, they are under the Azores high pressure, so it rarely rains. Since the islands are near the tropic of Cancer, the sun is nearly at its zenith during the months of June and July, offering the greatest and coolest UV exposure possible."

This is why most of us earthlings don't quite get scientists. They often speak somewhere in the ozone. But there is a very practical reason for this. *Scientists believe in scientific methods* (duh!). Scientific methods involve systematically studying data to reach conclusions that are, for the most part, accepted as factual and beyond reproach. They rely on research to guide their thinking—research involving observation, measurement, and manipulation of "real stuff" to come up with reasonably reliable conclusions.

If there was a phrase that would capture the essence of scientific BS, it would be "I appreciate what I validate" (or "I really don't care what you think. Prove it").

Scientific methods begin as simple thoughts. These thoughts may have limited evidence to back them up. They're raw and without real form. In their early stage, they're merely strongly held, unproven opinions. To become credible, they must be proven. They are proven through a systematic process of testing.

Most of us are more inclined to use gut reactions than scientific methods to form an opinion. We rely on our feelings and emotions more than logical reasoning. Why? you may ask. It's simple (yet complex). Our feelings are emotional responses to things we've taken a lifetime to create. We don't necessarily know where they come from—they just are what they are. They are something we don't have to think about because we already accept them as being true. So in our minds, there is no need to verify. Why relitigate? The work has already been done and the judgment rendered. No need to expend further time, energy, or effort.

The scientific approach is a little different. Scientific methods usually begin where gut reactions end. Gut reactions in the scientific scheme of things are comparable to unsubstantiated hypotheses. They're basically simple explanations of something with very little evidence to support it—you know, like the earth is flat. Hypotheses are often first reactions. However, in scientific circles they aren't accepted as "true" until they have been validated through a rigorous process of experimentation. Consequently, scientists view their gut reactions as the beginning of a process. This involves collecting data, running tests, making observations, and taking relevant measurements. They do whatever it takes to either prove or disprove their hypothesis. The purest among them do this with a minimum of judgment or bias. Their only goal is to reach a conclusion that is true—or at least solid by most reasonable standards.

The scientific approach is also strengthened by challenge. Any relevant question that can't be answered from previous research causes the scientist to start the investigative process all over again. Any relevant information not taken into consideration during the original research causes the true scientist to start the process all over again. So research is an iterative process.

Scientific methods don't make moral judgments or answer questions about values. These methods are designed specifically to build and test new ideas with the ultimate goal of creating new and reliable knowledge.

Data is obviously critical to the scientific process. Data is used to support any scientific assertion. Data can either be consistent with an assertion without ruling out apposing assertions, or it can provide direct validation of a single assertion. When we build something, we construct it step-by-step. Like a house, the strength of the structure that we build depends on the strength of its foundation. If the foundation is weak or built on unstable ground, the structure will ultimately fall.

Scientific methods build scientific knowledge. This knowledge is usually accepted as "fact"—considered to be valid and true. But are they really? Maybe, maybe not. Since theories are developed by people, they can also inadvertently include people's biases. For instance, proponents of medical marijuana argue that it can be a safe and effective treatment for the symptoms of cancer, AIDS, multiple sclerosis, pain, glaucoma, epilepsy, and other conditions. They cite dozens of peer-reviewed studies, prominent medical organizations, major government reports, and the use of marijuana as medicine throughout world history.

Opponents of medical marijuana argue that it is too dangerous to use, lacks FDA approval, and that various legal drugs make marijuana use unnecessary. They say marijuana is addictive, leads to harder drug use, interferes with fertility, impairs driving ability, and injures the lungs, immune system, and brain. They say that medical marijuana is a front for drug legalization and recreational use (ProCon.org).

So the question is, can medical marijuana be an effective treatment for MS, epilepsy, and glaucoma *and* at the same time be addictive and injurious to lungs and immune system. The obvious answer is, yes, it can. These can all be "scientific, proven through a rigorous process of validation." However, depending on your personal feeling about medical marijuana usage, you will most likely choose the "scientific facts" that support what you already believe.

A common bias associated with scientific BS type is *data bias*. Data bias has an impact on the quality of data selected to prove a given hypothesis. The choice of data used can drive competing theories, can be used to make moral judgments, but can't answer questions about values. One of the deficiencies in the scientific approach is inadequate testing. This leads us to the risks associated with scientific BS. The data selected can lead to false results. In scientific research, data selection involves choosing data for analysis in such a way that it is a true test of the hypothesis. In order for the data to effectively test any hypothesis, it must be random or unpredictable. If you can predict the outcome of the test before testing, the data used was probably not chosen randomly. But it was instead chosen to drive some specific outcome. Consequently, the sampling doesn't represent the intended population. This form of bias is often referred to as "selection bias" and completely distorts any statistical analysis.

"Many businesses only capture a small piece of the pie when it comes to data available to their particular business segment, and this means their data and subsequent analysis are skewed." Statistical significance simply means that you are very sure that the statistics are adequate and reliable for testing the hypothesis. Suppose ten people are given an IQ test to determine the perspective differences between men and women. The group is composed of five women and five men. We find that the difference is .00001. What if there were 20,000 participants with a difference of .001, would the results be more significant? Of course, a larger sample size would obviously yield a more significant result. What about 100 participants with 90 women and 10 men—an obvious skewing of the data.

How about trying to determine the average US household income by collecting data only from Scarsdale, New York (Avg. household income $241,000 ++)? The data sampling is obviously inadequate to obtain the desired results.

Scientist (Empiricist)	Characteristics	Benefits	Limitations
Systematic investigation into and study of materials and sources in order to establish facts and reach new conclusions.	• Research-based BS • Evidence centered • Strategy driven	• Rational • Builds knowledge • Generates new ideas • Validates through iterative testing • Strengthened by challenge • Doesn't make moral judgments • Results are quantifiable, observation	• Can drive competing theories • Can be used to make moral judgments • Can't answer questions about values • Method deficiencies— inadequate testing

Mantra: "I appreciate what I validate."

Common Bias: Data Bias

Expert

The other day I heard a politician while being questioned aggressively essentially say "I admit I have very little experience in this area and know next to nothing about the subject, but in my expert opinion…" What? Who cares what you think. Not only is your opinion BS, it's also, by your own admission, uninformed BS.

The Cynical Web Site defines an expert, cynically of course, as "a person with more data than judgment" or "someone who knows a lot about something, and very little about anything else." There are an unlimited number of self-proclaimed experts in the world. Due diligence is invariably necessary to differentiate the experts from the pseudo-experts, who often look and sound very much alike. We've all met at least one know-it-all. Someone who knows exactly what you should do about parenting, dating, investing, and losing weight or anything else that might come to mind. Pseudo-experts are usually willing to share their opinions on any subject—whether they understand it or not. They provide high-level explanations with few facts to support them. Some pseudo-experts are great actors who pretend to know everything, while others have no idea how little they know. Being a pseudo-expert is really easy—it involves no personal risk. The risk falls on those who follow their advice.

The difference between scientists and experts is that scientists use specialized methods to develop scientific facts. Experts assimilate those facts to create rational theories. Using the house metaphor, scientists create the "bricks" that experts use to build the "walls." They collect relevant data and construct reasonable theories.

Real experts offer data-based evidence to support any assertions they make. They are capable of telling you what, why, and how something can, cannot, should, or should not be done. They provide performance standards and specific examples to explain any assertions they might make. Some experts can be so deeply immersed in their field that they may not even realize that most don't even know the basics of their area of expertise. They sometimes speak at a level beyond the comprehension of those they wish to engage. This leaves an opening for a well-spoken yet ill-informed pseudo-expert to secure undeserved credibility even over a true expert. So credibility is more a function of the perception of others—of a person's level of trust, believability, and confidence more so than their level of expertise in any given subject. The most effective experts understand the big picture and can find simple ways to explain complex concepts.

Real experts don't just have unsubstantiated opinions—they have proof that backs them up. They offer opinions based on some kind of knowledge, be it academic or experiential. However, I think we can all agree that the most credible experts have had some practical involvement in a given subject above and beyond just classroom learning. So generally, expertise is knowledge and experience based.

If this BS type had a personal mantra, it would probably be "I go with what I know" or "If I don't know, I make it up based on what I do know."

Not so long ago, the story of a missing airliner over the South China Sea dominated the news. Apparently, the planes signaling system (ACARS) had been disabled before the pilot's last conversations with an air traffic controller. During that exchange the pilot made no mention of any trouble.

- On March 8 the plane took off at 12:41 a.m. carrying 239 people headed for Beijing.

- The plane reached a cruising altitude of 35,000 feet at 1:01 a.m.
- At approximately 1:07 a.m., the plane sent its last ACARS message.
- The plane reached the east coast of the Malaysian Peninsula at about 1:08 a.m. according to an independent radar tracking system.
- A satellite picked up four or five signals from the plane after it left the range of military radar.
- These signals indicated that the plane had veered significantly off its original Beijing flight path.

The aforementioned were the facts as reported. From these facts, official investigators and aviation experts came up with numerous theories to explain what might have happened to the airliner. These theories were varied and bizarre. They included everything from a tragic midair explosion to mechanical problem to a meticulously planned midair hijacking.

So much BS, where do I begin?

There is a wonderful group activity that I used to conduct called the Great Debate. This activity involves creating two teams to debate with each other on a controversial topic of the day. Each is instructed to write a persuasive argument taking opposite sides of the chosen issue. Each team is given the same information. They are to state a clear position in either support or opposition to a proposal. They are to support their position with relevant evidence. They are to deliver informative presentations about an important idea, issue, or event by framing questions to direct the investigation, establishing a controlling idea or topic and developing the topic with simple facts, details, examples, and explanations. It's amazing how the same data can be used to support such divergent perspectives. That's why there will always be an abundance of experts to argue any side of a given issue. And sadly, as was the case with the missing airliner, most are wrong.

The effectiveness of an expert is contingent upon the expert's experience, skills, abilities, credentials, education, specialized knowledge, credibility, reliability, judgment, and analytic capabilities. The things that inhibit an expert's effectiveness aside from the absence of the aforementioned characteristics are personal biases and preferences, self-righteous judgments, disregard for the expertise of others, and misuse of their expert "authority."

A common bias associated the expert BS type is *preference bias*. A preference bias is where the expert is predisposed or has a preference for using one tool or one approach over another. In fact, the more experience an expert has in any given area, the more difficult it is for them to utilize less familiar tools and approaches or break preferred approaches down into their component parts so that others might understand. According to Prof. Jonah Gelbach of the University of Chicago Law School, the way we see a problem is often skewed by the type of tool we have to solve it. "The tools we are able to apply to a problem often alters our perception of the problem we face and the solutions that are appropriate."

Expert (Specialist)	Characteristics	Advantages	Disadvantages
Offer experience based opinions based on practical involvement with or observation of a given subject.	• Knowledge-based BS • Expertise centered • Experience driven	• Breadth of experience • Skills and abilities • Credentials, education • Specialized learned knowledge • Considered credible and reliable • Capable of greater depth of analysis • Trusted judgment • Acts in response to particular situations rather than upon abstract ideals	• Personal biases, preferences • Qualifications, knowledge Limitations • Righteous judgments • Disregard of expertise of others • Misuse of expert "authority"
Mantra: "I go with what I know."			
Common Bias: Preference bias			

Pundits

A pundit is generally defined as a person who offers opinions or commentary on a particular subject that they may or may not have expert knowledge of. Being an expert is not a prerequisite to being a pundit. By definition, anyone with an opinion can potentially qualify as a pundit. Consequently, there's no shortage of pundits to critique everything from politics to entertainment, to sports, to current events, to science and technology, and on and on and on.

Tom Van Riper, a contributor to *Forbes* magazine, once said that Cable news networks try to one-up each other by rolling out programs that are hosted by people with strong, even if illogical positions on any given subject. These pundits love going one-on-one with guests who also bring strong views to the table. If you want to stand out from the media clutter, bring a strong point of view and, at least, pretend you're an expert.

So pundits are not necessarily experts on a given topic. *The difference between pundits and experts is that experts use knowledge to build theories and pundits present their opinions as though it were knowledge.* Pundits are more often than not people with more judgment than wisdom. They can even be someone who knows a little about a lot of things and less about everything else. Extending the house metaphor, scientists create the "bricks," experts use the bricks to build the walls, and pundits add color to those walls.

Most credible pundits are rated highly on awareness, oratory skills, or general likability measurements. Those that are successful generally establish a strong emotional connection with their viewers. A pundit is usually a public figure whose primary focus is bringing opinions and commentary to political, legal, sports, entertainment, and other issues. The best pundits are able to check their personal views at the door when talking to politicians or celebrities who are pushing their particular causes.

Many experts often successfully make the jump to punditry. The trick is having a wide enough appeal to draw a large audience. Though television still rules as a major outlet for the opinions of the numerous pundits, new social media such as Facebook, Twitter, Instagram, and others are continually gaining momentum.

Those who are fortunate enough to become successful pundits are perceived by the public as intelligent, experienced, and articulate, whether true or not. If your voice can rise above the crowd in a smart and articulate way, you might have a shot at becoming a successful pundit. It's more difficult for political pundits to secure widespread appeal because they generally bring a biased label such as liberal or conservative. This draws cheers from half the population and jeers from the other half.

The following excerpt is also from the Cynical Web Site-"Thank Gawd for cynical people whose anchor in hard-won reality keep starry-eyed idealists from causing real trouble. America is awash in cynics, a byproduct of American pioneer upbringing and a perpetual slate of candidates that provide cynics fresh meat (as if they needed more, those intellectual gluttons). Yet even among cynics, some are held in awe for their acerbic observations and verbal eviscerations. Cynics elevate them to divine heights, though real cynics see that as a profit-making ploy. We suspect that master cynics stand apart because their disparaging and blasphemous prose made them prime candidate for eradication, either by unhappy public figures or by the alleged Almighty himself. Regardless of the reason, we see these individuals as exceptionally gifted in the art of rupturing self-inflated egos, sarcastically smashing revered icons, and generally sneering at everything that mortals hold sacred. In these pages, we present some biographical information on these despots of disrepute and provide their pearls of wanton wisdom from our ever growing database."

I'm happy we have cynics who have a realistic perspective that balances the fantasy world of some opportunist and idealist.

If this BS type had a personal mantra, it would probably be "I believe what I conceive."

Good pundits are skilled "reasoners" and can make even the unreasonable seem plausible. Reasoners are good at finding evidence that supports positions they already hold (usually for intuitive reasons). They can be open-minded and truth-seeking in the absence of self-interest or reputational concerns. ("Can I believe it?" / "Must I believe it?") Their judgment is beyond reproach. Their credibility is based on the overwhelmingly positive perception of who they are and the irrefutable belief in what they know.

Effective pundits are able to make informed choices based on personal observations and make logical connections between facts to come up with reasonable ideas and practical explanations. Some downsides of punditry are that many pundits are "talking heads" and lack personal knowledge. Many also deal with things based on hypothetical considerations and creative rationalizations.

Confirmation bias is the tendency to favor new information that confirms a preexisting belief. This implies giving disproportionately less consideration to alternative beliefs. This type of cognitive bias is a form of inductive reasoning. People display this bias when they gather or remember information selectively, or when they interpret it in a biased way. The effect is stronger for emotionally charged issues and for deeply entrenched beliefs.

Pundits (Rationalist)	Characteristics	Advantages	Disadvantages
Develop theories or systems of ideas intended to explain something, often based on general principles independent of the thing to be explained.	• Logic-based BS • Credibility centered • Judgment-driven	• Logical assertions • Theorizes based on observed phenomena • Uses reasoning to come up with practical ideas	• "Talking heads" • Personal credibility can supersede knowledge • Dealing with things based on hypothetical considerations
Mantra: "I believe what I conceive."	Reasoners are good at finding evidence to support the positions they already hold (usually for intuitive reasons). Can be open-minded and truth seeking in the absence of self-interest or reputational concerns. ("Can I believe it?" / "Must I believe it?")	• Considers given facts and comes up with a possible explanation • Practical ideas	• Creative rationalizations (reasoning for a course of action or a particular belief)
Intelligence: people with higher IQs are able to generate more reasons—able to generate a greater number of "my-side" arguments that usually buttress their own cases rather than exploring the entire issue more fully and even handedly.			

Opportunist

An opportunist is defined as a person who exploits circumstances to gain immediate advantage rather than being guided by consistent principles or a plan. However, unlike most pundits, opportunists can also be self-absorbed, closed-minded and truth-avoiding in pursuit of self-interest or reputational concerns.

In a very funny cartoon created by Roy Delgado, two obviously prosperous businessmen are standing in a well-appointed office in a high-rise building looking out of the window. One, the obvious "dominant" of the two, is drinking what I assume to be an alcoholic beverage and smoking a cigar.

The dominant turns to the other and says, "I didn't believe in global warming…until I found a way to make money at it."

Many social scientists tell us that intelligent people are able to generate more reasons to support any given position they decide to take. Given any amount of data, they are able to generate more "my-side" arguments to reinforce their own case. They are even able to create reasonable sounding arguments without fully exploring the entire issue at hand. A creative mind can generate an abundance of arguments with very little data.

In the book *Animal Farm* written by Eric Blair, better known as George Orwell, there's a character named Squealer, who was the farm's fictional minister of propaganda and second-in-command to the farm's leader, Napoleon. Squealer's primary responsibility was to protect Napoleon's reputation and justify his actions, no matter how dishonest or deplorable. Today's politicians are amateurs compared to Squealer. He could weave a story that could convince others that garbage was gold, waste could replace needed sustenance, the unjust was just, and defeat was indeed victory. One example of Squealer's creative exploits was following the creation of the Animal Farm's infamous "Seven Commandments," one of which was that "All animals are equal." When an explanation was needed for the mysterious disappearance of excess apples and milk that the pigs had commandeered for their own personal consumption, Squealer was sent to explain. Squealer began by referring to the other farm animals as "Comrades!" (How inclusive and endearing.) He continues, "You do not imagine, I hope, that we pigs are doing this in the spirit of selfishness and privilege? Many of us—pigs—actually dislike milk and apples. Our sole objective in taking these things is to preserve our health. Milk and apples—this has been proved by science, comrades—contains substances absolutely necessary for the well-being of a pig. We pigs are brainworkers… Day and night we are watching over your welfare. It is for your sake that we drink milk and eat those apples. Do you know what would happen if we pigs failed in our duty? Jones [the farm's demonized owner who had been forced by the animals to abandon his property] would come back! Surely there is no one among you who wants to see Jones come back?" (Pure creative genius—if you're a pig! Evil, conniving deception if you're not.)

There are many Squealers active today. As a matter of fact, I heard one just the other day. It went something like this: "My fellow Americans!" (Once again, inclusive and endearing.) "You do not imagine, I hope, that we are passing this *tax cut* in the spirit of selfishness and privilege? Many of us will actually be hurt by this *tax cut*. Our sole objective in *cutting taxes* is to preserve the *health of the economy*. *Tax cuts for businesses and the wealthy*—this has been proven by *economists*—contains substances absolutely necessary to *stimulate business investment and job creation*. We *are the job creators*... Day and night we are watching over your welfare. It is for your sake that we *cut taxes*. Do you know what would happen if we failed in our duty? The *other party* would come back! Surely there is no one among you who wants to see the *other party* come back?"

The similarities are striking, are they not? The reason *Animal Farm* is such an enduring classic (copyrighted in 1946) is because it contains timeless truths about human nature. It is a simple story with complex meanings. To borrow from Oliver Wendell Holmes, it is "simplicity that lies on the other side of complexity."

This is the essence of opportunism. The opportunist begins with a goal and then finds the data that best supports it. For an opportunist, data is relevant, but only to the extent that it supports the opportunist's greater goal. So unlike the scientist whose single-minded goal is to validate facts using scientific methods, the opportunist seeks out facts that serve their goal. These facts are not necessarily relevant facts. For example, if somehow, through some freak of nature, it snows in Phoenix in July, this single piece of data might be used as "proof" by some that global warming doesn't exist. Yes, the snow in Phoenix in July would be a fact. But the burden of proof requires a much more rigorous process of validation. Two real world examples of political opportunism follow. Jennifer Sclafani, an associate professor at Georgetown University who studies the construction of political identity through language, says that a good story is linguistically sound. That is, it has a context, orientation, and real examples to support the narrative. It uses vivid imagery to help people to easily visualize and understand the narrative. Dr. Sclafani references a specific politician (who will remain nameless) who is very atypical—the "antipolitician," if you will. This particular political candidate ran a very successful campaign if the number of Twitter followers is any measure of success. Dr. Sclafani talks about his ability to tell an effective story. She says firstly that he begins his stories out of nowhere with no orientation, context, or setting of the scene. Regardless of the question he's asked, he begins by stating the topic to which he plans to respond. For example, if the question "What strategy would you use to combat an enemy on foreign soil" was asked, he would immediately shift the conversation to "security." Then "focus" the conversation on "securing our borders"—which is completely divorced from the original question. He would then go into a long, convoluted narrative about his recent visit to the border, selectively sharing (with emphasis, I might add) what he supposedly discovered from talking to the border guards. He gives no specifics—no date, time, location, name, or any other identifiable characteristics of "the guard" he talked to. This gives him complete freedom to say whatever he wants, be it true or not, without question or challenge (pure genius or pure deception). He then shifts from past to present tense to assure his listeners that he will fix the real or imagined problem he just shared, again with no specific or tangible actions he would take. He then implores his listeners to just "trust" him." He ends with the very decisive and conclusive declaration that's just the way it is—whether you like it or not. This statement is, at times, totally removed from the narrative.

"During a highly contested primary campaign one well known politician misinformed primary voters about the status of one of his rivals. In an effort to narrow the primary field and secure a rival's constituents, a senator's campaign falsely claimed that the rival planned to go to Florida after the next state primary, implying that the targeted rival was suspending his campaign, which in 'political speak' usually infers that a campaign is shutting down.

A reporter later revealed that the senator's rival would continue campaigning after taking a short break in Florida. When the senator was confronted with evidence of his misdeed, he claimed that it was the media's fault. The network that was accused responded with a strongly worded statement saying that the senator's claims were false and that at no point had the network indicated that his rival had suspended his campaign. Eventually the senator acknowledged that the news network got it right.

Though the senator seemed to acquiesce after the attempted deception was revealed, the senator's campaign aides continued to alert supporters that the rival's campaign was short-lived. In an attempt to save face, the senator's campaign said it didn't explicitly state that their rival was dropping out; they only implied it by telling their supporters to tell the rival's supporters that he was going on vacation. Later, an investigative reporter for a major news network found that even after the senator's misrepresentation was made public, a number of the rival's supporters continued to be told by the senator's campaign that the rival was indeed dropping out.

The moral of the story, when running for a public office, don't go to Florida."

When politicians compete for votes and money, there is often some amount of trickery or demagoguery involved. Politicians tend to play fast and loose with the truth, attempting to portray themselves as the hope for the future and their opponents as evil incarnate—each trying to influence public opinion to their advantage. Influencing others for personal, communal, or corporate gain is an act of opportunism.

Opportunism is characterized by a self-centered view of the world, a willingness to bend the rules, and a belief that the end justifies the means. Opportunists are self-serving, pragmatic, rational, creative, calculating, observant, and well informed—all of which allow them to see and take advantage of perceived opportunities. Opportunists are willing to abuse power and authority, sacrifice integrity, ignore ideals, and be manipulative and divisive, if necessary, to accomplish their desired goal. If this BS type had a personal mantra, it would probably be "I will defend what allows me to win."

Selection bias is a bias in which a sample is collected in such a way that some members of the intended population are less likely to be included than others. It results in a biased sample, a nonrandom sample of a population (or nonhuman factors) in which all individuals, or instances, were not equally likely to have been selected. If this is not accounted for, results can be erroneously attributed to the phenomenon under study rather than to the method of sampling. Medical sources sometimes refer to sampling bias as ascertainment bias. Ascertainment bias has basically the same definition but is still sometimes classified as a separate type of bias.

In 2014 a senator famously tossed a snowball on the Senate floor while claiming that global warming was a hoax. He cited recent unseasonably cold temperatures across the country as evidence that global warming claims were exaggerated. The evidence he used to support his claim was sixty-seven examples of new record lows occurring on a single day in various cities in the Northeastern and Midwestern United States. Even though weather-related data had been officially tracked for over a century, this particular senator sought to prove his point by using a small sampling of data that was a meteorological anomaly, ignoring over one hundred years that taken together painted quite a different picture.

Opportunist	Characteristics	Advantages	Disadvantages
The practice of influencing others for personal, communal or corporate gain.	• Power-based BS • Influence-centered • Goal-driven	• Pragmatic, rational • Effectively relies on group feedback	• Abuse of power and authority • Can be self-serving • Integrity can be sacrificed
Mantra: "I will always defend what allows me to win."	When politicians compete for votes and money, there will always	• Can create more unity and cooperation • Influences art	• Ideals can be ignored to accomplish the goals
Common Bias: Selection bias	be some level of trickery and demagoguery, as politicians play fast and loose with the truth, attempting to portray themselves in the best possible light and their opponents as fools that will lead the country into ruin.	and science of moving groups • Secures needed resources • Methods and tactics involving authority and power • Can break down resistance	• Opportunistic. • Can be manipulative • Can be divisive

Ideologues

The difference between an opportunist and an ideologue is that an opportunist uses selective data to make assertions and an ideologue makes assertions independent of data.

An assertion is merely a declaration that something is, in fact, true. Most political assertions are unable to withstand the burden of proof, which is why they are made so callously and irresponsibly. In the article "Why People Are Irrational about Politics," Michael Huemer says, "The most striking feature of the subject of politics is how prone it is to disagreement." He offers four possible theories for why political disagreements are so prevalent:

The first he calls the "miscalculation theory." Political issues are really difficult to understand, no matter how simple politicians try to make them sound. How often have you heard politicians say "If I'm elected, I'll eliminate racism, end war, support our allies, destroy our enemies, fix our economy…yada, yada, yada…bring prosperity to all." Think about the number of factors and calculations needed in making even one, let alone all these things, happen. It's like solving an unbelievably complex mathematical problem. It's real easy to make a miscalculation. So if everyone is doing their own calculations, it's highly probable that there will be many different results. This can obviously lead to disagreement.

The second he calls the "ignorance theory." This one is fairly straightforward. Unlike the miscalculation theory, the ignorance theory doesn't involve abstractness or complexity. It involves, well, ignorance! Ignorance is defined as a lack of knowledge or information. Political issues are often difficult to resolve because people might have either insufficient information or different information. This may be because they don't have access to more information or they've formed a conclusion and don't feel they need more information. Huemer also adds that people may not only be ignorant of the facts pertaining to an issue, but also ignorant of their own level of ignorance (don't know what they don't know). Consequently, this reinforces their confidence in the correctness of their political views.

However, it remains puzzling why people would be ignorant of their own level of ignorance.

The third is the "irrationality theory." People, in general, are irrational when it comes to politics. Rational thought usually means using logical reasoning to make a decision. Irrational is quite the opposite—neither logical nor reasonable. But what constitutes "logical reasoning" is debatable. One's personal preferences can be easily confused with rational thought. Usually people seek evidence to support what they already believe and resist any evidence to the contrary. Whereas many might argue that this is not "logical reasoning" because it ignores volumes of data that might be relevant to their choice. Those who selectively choose only data that support their position may, in turn, argue that it's the only data that is relevant to their choice—classic Joseph Heller catch-22. The bottom line is that when it comes to politics, we are often rationally irrational—we lean toward what "pleases" us first (subjectively irrational) and why it pleases us second (objectively rational). Huh…?

The fourth is the "divergent-values theory." People often disagree about politics because they have fundamentally different values. Their choices often revolve around personal moral standards or individual values. This is quite evident when you bring up topics that have historically been froth with controversy such as abortion, affirmative action, gay rights, capital punishment, global warming, stem cell research, Christianity, and many others. An employer who (subconsciously) prefers male employees may rationalize his disproportionately high number of male staff members by saying he was unable to find any qualified female applicants. Subsequently, a formal review of hiring practices might reveal that female applicants, though qualified, were systematically excluded from the hiring process. The question is, "was this a conscious process of exclusion or not?"

After reading this, you may be asking, "Is being an ideologue a bad thing?" It would be inappropriate for me to call all Ideologues miscalculating, ignorant, irrational, value driven zealots. But many are. Ideologues may not be on the extreme end of all these theories. But they are often extreme in one or more. They may miscalculate based on faulty assumptions. They may be ignorant based on insufficient information. They may be irrationally influenced by strongly held moral beliefs or personal values.

All these things together won't necessarily make you an ideologue. What locks you in the ideologue bucket is what happens after you discover that you've made a miscalculation, chosen incorrect or irrelevant data, relied more on feelings than logic and rationale, or allowed your personal values to desensitize you to the perspectives of others. Firstly, would you be willing to acknowledge any "misconceptions" that are brought to your attention? Secondly, would you actively seek to reexamine your position and be open to change if your position is found untenable? If your answer to each of these questions is no and you are either unwilling or unable to even consider examining any possible deficiencies in your thinking, then you're probably an ideologue.

Rachana Pradhan's article on Kentucky's attempt to dismantle the Affordable Care Act captures the essence of a true ideologue. Rachana writes

> "Kentucky's new Republican governor is plowing ahead with plans to close down the state-run Obamacare insurance marketplace, shuttering an exchange that the White House had hailed as a model for the law's success. Gov. Matt Bevin recently notified the Obama administration that he will dismantle Kentucky's enrollment website, which worked nearly glitch-free when the Obama administration and other states bungled Obamacare's launch in 2013. The decision marks the first time a state will scrap a functional state-run marketplace to join the federal enrollment site, HealthCare.gov, which has been working much more smoothly since its initial rollout. Bevin campaigned on repealing the state-based exchange, known as Kynect and built with nearly $300 million in federal grants, calling the marketplace redundant when the federal government

oversees Obamacare enrollment for 38 states. The Republican governor, however, has retreated from his earlier calls for repealing the state's Medicaid expansion and now says he wants to overhaul the program that has covered roughly 400,000 low-income adults. Bevin's health care decisions come as a disappointment to supporters who viewed the state as the Obamacare jewel of the South, where most states remain ardently opposed to the health care law. Former Democratic Gov. Steve Beshear's decision to expand coverage through executive orders helped Kentucky record one of the largest statewide drops in the uninsured rate in the past two years."

Ideologues are usually immediately accepting of things that they feel are consistent with their ideological stand without the need for conscious reasoning. That's because they are, according to *Merriam-Webster*, "often blindly partisan advocates or adherents of a particular ideology." By definition, they are blindly partisan.

The partisan mind seeks reinforcement from the outside world. When we want to believe something, we ask ourselves, "Can I believe it?" Then we begin the search for evidence to support what we already want to believe. The partisan mind uses this biased evidence to reinforce its partisan beliefs and block out any unwanted contradictory beliefs. Soon "a false conception and persistent belief unconquerable by reason" emerges.

Ideologues are characterized by obsessive enthusiasm, elevated involvement, abiding devotion, and obsessive belief in an ideology. They are guided more by ideals than by practical considerations—ideals that are not necessarily supported by facts. They often have little tolerance for contrary ideas and are self-confirming in their thinking. (Meaning, they search, interpret, or recall information in a way that confirms their beliefs.) Ideals adopted by ideologues can be contrary to social and political norms. If this BS type had a personal mantra, it would probably be "I won't be led astray by any other way" or "I know the way and will not be led astray."

To be ideologically biased is to be influenced to see your reality from only a particular viewpoint. In other words, ideological bias is the collection of ideas or beliefs, held by an individual or a group of people. They may be the whole society or just a portion of that society. Political parties each have an ideology they generally adhere to and espouse. This makes their views ideologically biased. All humans are biased in one form or another. The best thing, in my opinion, is to examine all viewpoints and try to choose the best from each, rather than accepting one with no thought. "A great many people will think they are thinking when they are merely rearranging their prejudices" (William James).

Projection bias refers to a general assumption that 1) you will feel the same about something in the future as you do today, and 2) that others feel the same as you do. As individuals, we are trapped in our own heads twenty-four hours a day. It's often difficult for us to project outside the bounds of our own consciousness and preferences. We tend to assume that most people think just like us—though there may be no justification for it. This cognitive shortcoming often leads to a related effect known as the false consensus bias where we tend to believe that people not only think like us, but that they also agree with us. It's a bias where we overestimate how typical and normal we are and assume that a consensus exists on matters when there may be none. Moreover, it can also create the effect where the members of a radical or fringe group assume that more people on the outside agree with them than is the case. Or the exaggerated confidence one has when predicting the winner of an election or sports match.

Ideologues (Idealist)	Characteristics	Advantages	Disadvantages
The ability to understand something immediately without the need for conscious reasoning. **Mantra:** "I won't be deceived by what others believe. Nor will I be led astray by what others might say."	• Intuition-based BS • Belief-centered • Cause-driven A false conception and persistent belief unconquerable by reason in something has no existence in fact. When we want to believe something we ask ourselves "Can I believe it?" Then we search for supporting evidence. The partisan brain has been reinforced so many times for performing mental contortions that free it from unwanted beliefs.	• Idealist— belief-based • Idealist • Uncritical zeal • Obsessive enthusiasm • Elevated involvement, devotion, obsession to a cause	• Guided more by ideals than by practical considerations • Can be unsupported by facts • Can lose sight of goal • Little tolerance for contrary ideas or opinions • Self-confirming— search for, interpret, or recall information in a way that confirms one's beliefs • Can be contrary to social and political norms • Lack of compromise • Excessive unyielding devotion to a cause

There can be a loose correlation between your preferred style of storytelling and your predisposition to using facts.

- For scientists, exploring the largest domain of available facts is essential. Their purpose is to inform and investigate. Scientist—technocrats—designs; scientist, engineers, technologists (facts).
- For experts, relevant facts are needed to substantiate their specific area of expertise. Their purpose is to instruct and analyze. Experts—strategists—direct election campaign; expertise bias (specialty/specialization).

- For pundits, select facts are used to support their theories. Their purpose is to inquire and theorize. Pundits—analysts—implements plans (rationale/rationalization).

- For opportunists, any fact that serves their purpose. Their purpose is to influence and capitalize. Opportunists—exploitation—removes obstacles (advantage / goal attainment).

- For ideologues, only facts support their ideology. Their purpose is to inspire and prescribe. Ideologues—believers—secure commitments (philosophy/uncompromising).

If the types are placed on a continuum from the most fact-dependent to the least, it may look something like this:

Scientist	Expert	Pundit	Opportunist	Ideologue
Fact	Rationale	Opinion	Construct	Belief
Validates facts through scientific methods.	Uses facts to solve problems.	Uses facts to explore options.	Uses selective facts to gain advantage.	Uses selective facts that support beliefs.

The term *proportionality* generally refers to the amount of evidence needed to prove the "truthfulness" of any given assertion. An assertion is considered to be "true" if there is an "adequate" amount of evidence to support it. "True" and "adequate" are in quotations because they can always be questioned no matter how much evidence there is to support an assertion. Though truth is elusive, facts are less so.

- An extraordinary amount of evidence (or strong faith) is needed to support an extraordinary assertion (e.g., Jesus died for the sins of mankind).

- A reasonable amount of evidence (or strong rationale) is needed to

115

support a logical assertion (e.g., Tiger Woods was the best golfer in the history of the PGA.)

- Very little evidence (or strong belief) is needed to support a general assertion that is based on a recurring physiological occurrence (e.g., the sun will rise tomorrow).

You can see the potential challenges that might arise in conversations involving different BS types. Take the following examples:

- An "ideologue" may want to talk about the strength of their belief in equal justice because "it's only right," while an "expert" may want to know "how the ideologue defines equal justice and what evidence they have that it is not equal?" The ideologue may respond with a few anecdotal examples of what they believe to be acts of injustice, and the expert may produce a study with fifty thousand participants (exaggerated for affect) that concludes something quite different than the ideologue's assertion. The ideologue will immediately dismiss the study as being "wrong," and the expert will immediately dismiss the ideologues beliefs as unsubstantiated.

- An "opportunist" may boast of his support of an initiative to feed the needy based on his recent contribution to a local food pantry. After some research, a "scientist" might point out that his contribution was less than a third of the average contribution while his income was more than triple the average income of those who contributed. The "scientific fact finder" might ask how the "opportunistic giver" defines "support," and the "opportunist" might (defensively) respond that any gift, no matter how small, is evidence of support.

- A "pundit" might say that the *Windy City Blowhards* who recently won the International Crap Shooting Contest were the best crap shooters in the history of crap shooting. Another "pundit" might say "No, that's not true. The best crap shooting team of all times was the *Twin City Crappers* who won the championship back in 2010." A "scientist" might say "that based on my study of all crap-shooting contests and teams that have participated domestically and internationally, inception-to-date, using the officially sanctioned International Crap Standards, the best crap-shooting team of all times was the *Toledo High Crappers*, who won three successive international championships in the mid-1980s.

Conversations between people with differing approaches to BS present unique challenges. The following chart attempts to summarize some of those challenges.

	Scientist	Expert	Pundit	Opportunist	Ideologue
Scientist	**Facts** Variant *lines of evidence*	Specialized expertise (analysis) competes with scientific knowledge (facts)	Rationalizations (interpretations) compete with scientific knowledge (facts)	Goal attainment (advantage) competes with scientific knowledge (facts)	Philosophy (beliefs) compete with scientific knowledge (facts)
Expert	Scientific knowledge (facts) competes with specialized expertise (analysis)	**Rationale** Differing *specializations*	Rationalizations (interpretations) compete with specialized expertise (analysis)	Goal attainment (advantage) competes with specialized expertise (analysis)	Philosophy (beliefs) compete with specialized expertise (analysis)
Pundit	Scientific knowledge (facts) competes with rationalizations (interpretations)	Specialized expertise (analysis) competes with rationalization (interpretations)	**Opinion** Conflicting *interpretations*	Goal attainment (advantage) competes with rationalization (interpretations)	Philosophy (beliefs) compete with rationalizations (interpretations)
Opportunist	Scientific knowledge (facts) competes with goal attainment (advantage)	Specialized expertise (analysis) competes with goal attainment (advantage)	Rationalizations (interpretations) compete with goal attainment (advantage)	**Construct** Competing *goals and objectives*	Philosophy (beliefs) compete with goal attainment (advantage)
Ideologue	Scientific knowledge competes (facts) competes with philosophy (beliefs)	Specialized expertise (analysis) competes with philosophy (beliefs)	Rationalizations (interpretations) compete with philosophy (beliefs)	Goal attainment (advantage) competes with philosophy (beliefs)	**Belief** Divergent *beliefs*

Stories flow naturally from both facts and beliefs. Facts exist whether we acknowledge them as such or not. As stated previously, when something happens we automatically create stories to explain it. The thing that happens is a fact. The facts are then filtered through our beliefs and are thusly molded into stories. Again, the stories created are not always "true," and rarely do they take all facts into consideration. So *what we do, more often than not, is selectively choose facts that support what we already believe or what we want to convince others to believe.*

The measure of a story's success is not always whether it's right or wrong, good or bad, or true or false, but whether it accomplishes its intended purpose. Who decides that purpose? None other than the story's creator. I would venture to guess that most people judge stories of others by the accuracy of its content. On the other hand, they judge their own by their perception of how well it accomplishes its intended purpose. So the virtues of honesty and integrity are not necessarily the goals of all created stories. For instance, a story created to entertain, satirize, or dramatize may play a little fast and loose with the facts. However, a story created to document, instruct, or memorialize may be a bit more reliant on factual accuracy.

*****

When there are competing perspectives, it can become particularly disconcerting if there is also a power dynamic at play, or one person has substantially more power than the other. This is of particular concern when power has the potential to impact your livelihood or wellbeing as in the case of politics, business, and even religion. Does the person in power allow the disparate stories to coexist or do they force their version of the story (or their BS if you will) onto others?

Power in the sense that people like to be able to influence others. Control in that they don't want others to have undue influence over them. Influence, or the power to affect how others might think and act, is inherently biased. Depending on the source and strength of influence, its affects can span a broad network of individuals, subgroups and communities.

Stories don't just have power. They are the essence of power. Stories can drive the thoughts and actions of individuals and nations. They can lead to peace or war, prosperity or destruction, morality or decadence. Biases are part of the reality of our stories. They are reflections of our uniqueness, intrigue, and creativity.

I am in no way opposed to BS. But what I am an advocate of is being honest and intentional about the BS we choose to believe— whether it's of our own creation or others. What I call responsible BS. But more importantly, intentionally responsible for the BS that we create ourselves and sensitive to the impact that it has on others. (Divergent stories can and do coexist. They only do so in a free and open society that doesn't suppress differences.)

*****

I've observed (and participated in) many discussions where one party is quoting what in their mind is an indisputable fact from a highly reputable source, and the other is obviously making it up as they go along. When asked for facts to substantiate their position, they either aggressively challenge the facts presented by their adversary (deny your facts), reference some questionable source (displace), or worst case, make up a "fact" that supports their position; deny ("That's not true!"), displace ("What about Harry?"), disregard ("I don't care"), distort (use questionable or knowingly false "facts").

It is often impossible to see past our own intensely held beliefs in order to objectively weigh the facts of differing perspectives.

Scientist and experts—the major problem with our polarized political culture is that it fails to square with divergent views of the world. Scientist live their lives forward, collecting evidence, and going where the facts lead, with no mechanism or fervor to predict the outcome. Any resultant conclusions are based on an independent review of the information collected in its entirety, not on a desired outcome formulated from the start.

Ideologues—by contrast, in politics and religion, one starts with a desired outcome or strongly held belief and then seeks to find data that supports that predetermined conclusion. Whether it's electing a particular candidate, passing legislation, or defeating an enemy, every effort is calibrated to make the best use of resources, personnel, and public opinion in order to help one side win.

These two realities collide when someone hoping for a particular political outcome looks to law enforcement as the means to that end.

I witness similar conversations daily ("Trust me…they happen all the time"). These conversations have the potential to either escalate out of control or open up some new insights that may have never otherwise been realized. The key is to be aware of your tendencies, to not get sucked into the "rightness" of your perspective and to realize that it's all BS, anyway!

Section 5: The Tale the Teller Told

- ❖ Scientist BS
  - ➤ Systematically investigate hypotheses to establish new facts.
  - ➤ Research-based, evidence centered, and strategy driven.

- ❖ Expert BS
  - ➤ Offer experience-based opinions based on their knowledge of a given subject.
  - ➤ Knowledge-based, expertise centered, and experience driven.

- ❖ Pundit BS
  - ➤ Develop theories or ideas to explain something (e.g. event, action, etc.)
  - ➤ Logic-based, credibility centered, and judgment driven.

- ❖ Opportunist BS
  - ➤ Influence others for personal, communal or corporate gain.
  - ➤ Power-based BS, influence centered, and goal driven.

- ❖ Ideologue B
  - ➤ Rely on strongly held beliefs or intuition to formulate judgements.
  - ➤ Intuition-based, belief centered, and cause driven.

VI. Words: The Tools of Expression

Words are the building blocks of expression. Multiword sequences create narratives that express both simple and complex thoughts and ideas. So the choice of words and the sequence in which they are used is obviously important in story creation.

Words matter! They are used to convey thoughts and ideas to others. They can stand alone in a simple sentence (e.g., "Stop!," "Look," "Wait," "Why," "Delicious," "No," "Please," "Thanks") or be part of a complex sentence structure. Words have sensory characteristics of their own. They create sensations that can subconsciously stimulate our thinking and quickly render judgments. Some words generate a strong response instantly (arousal). While others we respond to with passive interest or no interest at all. The intensity of the arousal or interest in various words differs from person to person. If someone hears a word that they either don't understand or define differently, the intended message the word is trying to convey can be confused or distorted and the meaning of the message blurred.

Many words are complex "stories" that have evolved over time. Their meanings have been homogenized, fortified, and normalized in our personal lexicons (I think that means whenever we use the word it means the same thing). So if we hear someone use the word in a way that is unfamiliar, we generally have an immediate visceral reaction that says "that's not what that word means." For instance, if someone says "I have empathy for the homeless. That's why I voted for a homeless shelter to be built on the west side of the city [and of course, I live on the east side]," my first reaction would be, "What? Did you say, 'empathy'? Not my kind of empathy."

Words are sensations that arouse our imagination. Each time a word is spoken, we very quickly conjure up an impression of its significance and meaning. For example, a word as simple as "the" can create the sensation of anticipation of something to follow. Even if you said just the word "the" to a four- or five-year-old who was just beginning to explore the fundamentals of reading, they would say "the what?" Because they would immediately realize that in their experience, something always follows the "the" (the cat, the mouse, the hat, the rat, the boat, the fish...).

Each word obviously has its unique definition. But many words can have several different meanings. That's why dictionaries not only give a descriptive statement of a word's meaning, but they also use the word in a sentence and provide synonyms. Using the word in a sentence provides context. Synonyms are a list of words that have similar meanings. For instance, take the word *gregarious* (why? I have no idea). The most common usage of the word means "a sociable person." Words that have similar meanings are *friendly*, *outgoing*, *amiable*, *affable*, etc. A lesser known use of the word is "plants that grow in open clusters" or "animals who live in flocks" (who knew?). What if you were walking in the forest with a group of friends and came upon one of these clustered plants and said "those plants are gregarious." What do you think your friends would say? I can only imagine. *Gregarious* is just an interesting word that has very little meaning to me. As a matter of fact, though I know the commonly used definition and I'm quite capable of using it properly in a sentence, I have probably never used it before in my entire life (until now). I'm more of a "friendly," "outgoing," and even "amiable" than gregarious kind of guy.

You may be thinking, "So what?" Who cares whether a word has some obscure meaning? Well, you may not care whether gregarious has multiple meanings. But what about words that you do care about, like family, humility, love, compassion, integrity, justice, empathy, loyalty, or patriotism? How important is it to you that others understand what you mean when you use them? Let's take the word *humility*, for example. What synonyms come to mind when you hear the word *humility*? Do you think *weak*, *unassertive*, and *submissive*? Or do you think *introspective, altruistic,* and *unselfish*? Personally, I tend to lean toward the latter, as you can probably tell. But in isolation, it's only a word. We not only get to choose but, in reality, often do choose the meaning that we prefer. This sort *of word bias is where all our BS begins.*

Why are words so complex even in their simplicity? How can we hear the same thing yet hear it so differently? If we look the words up in a dictionary, won't that clear everything up? As I said before, a dictionary only provides a baseline of information about a word—its definitional content and meaning. However, our understanding and usage of the word is less about *content* than it is about *context*. As stated previously, words used in a specific narrative contextualizes their meaning. That's why most definitions not only give the variant descriptions of a word, but also use each in a sentence.

"I have a date," it may mean that you have a real hot cutie (generic male or female) lined up for a night on the town. Or it may mean that you have a delectable edible fruit in your possession that you can't wait to consume. Knowing which "date" is being referred to is obviously important in understanding the meaning of the state-ment. Each conjures up completely different images; you with the man or woman of your dreams or you seated at the table with a bowl of dried fruit. You can easily see how this can be very problematic if the speaker is referring to fruit and the hearer is thinking about a lovely young lady (my obvious preference again is door number two).

Just as there can be differing definitions for simple words such as *date*, there can also be differing definitions for complex words such as *faith, justice, compassion,* and *racism*. What makes these words com-plex? Not only are the meanings of these words nuanced, but they are also intricately linked to our personal values. This makes them inherently biased. Rather than having one or two variant definitions of these words, you may have two hundred. If you ask a group of individuals to each give their definitions of these words, plus use each in a sentence, you will most likely end up with reasonably sim-ilar definitions but highly variant usages. Asking each to further give examples that fit their definitions will more than likely increase the divergence even more.

Words Can Be Deceiving

The following is a story. The events depicted in this story are fictitious. Any similarity to any person, living or dead, is merely intentional. "A well-known politician once famously claimed, 'We're going to win so much you're going to be sick and tired of winning." A very simple, straightforward, and easy-to-understand statement, right? Wrong! Though it seems counterintuitive, the simpler the statement, the more room it leaves for interpretation. "What are you talking about?" you may ask. Well, let me explain.

The statement was "We're going to win." What could be plainer than that? Let's look again at what was said and what might have been heard. He said, "We're going to win," not that "We're all going to win." This may seem picky, but it's an extremely important distinction. Let's explore the elements of this statement that make it complex despite its simplicity.

Let's start with the contraction "we're." First of all, "we" is a pronoun. It is used to refer to some sort of group that consists of the speaker together with "others." Here's where the confusion comes in. What "others" is the speaker referring to? Are they his audience his family, his friends, his cohorts, his political party, his advocacy group, some citizens, all citizens, another country, or any combination thereof? And how would you know? Well, you can't, unless the speaker tells you. And since there is no explanation of who the "we" are, the listener is left to his or her own discretion to decide. And this is the cool thing about allowing that ambiguity to fester; it gives the speaker complete anonymity and control over defining who that "we" might be. And he can change it any time he chooses.

I, the listener, might believe that the "we" he was talking about was his cronies and cohorts. Or I might even think that "I" was included in that "we" (sounds funny but it's what I intended to say). No matter what I choose to think, it doesn't matter. If I made the public assertion that the speaker meant one group (his family and cronies for instance), he can always claim that my assertion was false. Why? Because he never defined who "we" are. No matter how often I guess or how "true" my guess might be, the speaker can always say

I'm wrong, even if I'm right. This is a case of simplistic complexity (pun intended).

If "we" is never defined, anytime something "positive" happens, no matter which group is affected, the speaker can claim "we" won.

- If the stock market rises, "*we won!*" (Despite it positively affecting only a small percentage of the populous.)
- If the GDP growth increases for one month, "*we won!*" (Despite similar or lesser increases in past months.)
- If a piece of advocated legislation passes in the House of Representatives, "*we won!*" (Despite it dying in the Senate and never becoming law.)

So the real goal was never "to win" in the traditional sense, but only to paint a picture of the speaker as a "winner." You don't do that by defining who "we" are or what "winning" is. Noooooooo. That would give others a *metric* that they could later use to measure performance.

While that person's opposition might walk around loudly advocating the details of their platform, "we're" going to

- provide affordable healthcare for all! (Our speaker simply says, "Repeal and replace.")
- create good-paying, clean energy jobs! (Our speaker simply says, "Grow the economy.")
- pursue our innovation agenda: science, research, education, and technology! (Our speaker simply says, "Improve education.")
- rein in Wall Street! (Our speaker simply says, "Drain the swamp.")
- make the wealthy pay their fair share of taxes! (Our speaker simply says, "Tax cuts for everybody.")

His opposition walks around baffled, exclaiming, "He hasn't said anything!" or "He hasn't done anything!" The pundits hammer him daily for not understanding the complexities of the job. But what they don't understand is that his goal was never to understand the complexities of the job or, for that matter, do anything meaningful. His goal was simply to be seen as a "winner." In order to do that, he had to fortify himself against criticism while simultaneously elevating the vulnerability of his opponents to criticism. How does he do that?

- *Provide* no *details.*

They only foster accountability. Let my opponents get mired in explaining the details of their proposals that only they understand. As for me, I'll tell my "peeps" what they need to know when they need to know it. They don't want to hear all that detail stuff anyway. They only need to know that "I'm a winner" and "we're going to win" (KISS—keep it simple stupid).

- *Criticize the details that others provide.*

Use what they give you to highlight their vulnerabilities. Keep them talking about what they're going to do, how much experience they have, and how much they know. The more detail, the better. Little Red Riding Hood—my, you have big teeth, better to bite you with, my dear.

- *When you win, claim victory. When you lose, claim victory. If you don't know whether you've won or loss, claim victory.*

Since I didn't give you any detail to define winning or losing, guess what, *we won!* Feed the flames of "we're winning" at all cost. Don't tolerate any comments to the contrary. Only share poll results that show that you're a winner (no matter how unreliable or dated they are). Employ the dynamics of war—we only had 5 million casualties. The good news is, *we won!*

Words Can Be Enlightening

When I think of the word winner, there are many that I can name off the top of my head that are "achievement-based" such as Nobel Prize winner, NBA champion, Super Bowl champion, Academy Award winner, poet laureate, etc. Other achievement-based generic categories might include elements of wealth, honor, position, status, or feats. Other distinctions around the word winner might be "character-based." These might include popular, warm, caring, compassionate, humble, or altruistic. All involve some earned reputational or goal-oriented accomplishment.

The word *winner*, for some, may strictly mean numerical dominance—more points, more money, more recognition, better grades, higher ratings, etc. Those who achieve these measured goals are usually rewarded by being given the moniker of "victor," "champion," "conqueror," "winner," or "the greatest of all times!" (Sorry, there was only one of those, and that would be *the* greatest of all time, Mohammed Ali. There is no bias in this story. It's just the pure unadulterated *truth!*)

Can these disparate definitions of the word *winner* coexist in the real world? Of course they can. But they, unfortunately, rarely do. There are many people who have notable achievements in their lives and are of good report and high moral standing. However, when we think of their success, we usually think in terms of either achievement or character, usually not both at the same time. When we think of Bill Gates, we think, "He's got a lot of money," and oh, by the way, he contributes a lot to charity. When we think of Mother Theresa, we think, "She's a really compassionate person who, for the better portion of her life, served the poor and needy of Calcutta." By the way, "she was poor." While everyone has heard of the philanthropic generosity of Bill Gates and the worthy sacrifices of Mother Theresa, has anyone heard of billionaire philanthropist Chuck Feeney? Chuck Feeney, while enormously wealthy, insisted on doing his philanthropy discreetly. One article reported that he had already given as much as $6.2 billion to philanthropic causes worldwide and had plans to give away the remaining $1.3 billion before he dies (Huh? No, you didn't misread. But I'm sure you might have your own thoughts.) If indeed he gave away his remaining $1.3 billion and was left penniless for the rest of his life, would you consider him a lunatic loser (with a capital *L*) or ultrasuccessful winner (with a capital *W*)? How many of us have fantasized about what we would do if we won the lottery? I'm sure for most of us, giving it all away wouldn't be high on the list of the choices we would consider.

Regardless of the life Mr. Feeney lived, I believe I would have to think of him more in terms of Mother Theresa than Bill Gates—the "sacrificial giver" versus the "billionaire philanthropist." The wonderful thing is that "we get to decide which story we want to believe." The disruptive thing is, "we get to decide which story we want to believe."

The meaning we ascribe to any word becomes our reference point for building further thought. Words (foundation—"a single distinct meaningful element of a narrative") / thoughts (context—"the circumstances that form the setting for an event") / narrative (structure—"a spoken or written account of connected events") / story (meaning—"an organized integrated whole that is important and worthwhile"). Materials (the base substance of what a thing is made of)…foundation (supports a structures load and provides stability)…frame (load bearing structure of the building)… house (a building created for human habitation). Cheap materials can create a weak foundation that will not properly support the frame and make the house unstable. Likewise, ambiguous words can create confusing thoughts that drive ambiguous narratives that produce ineffective stories. So precautions have to be taken in each step of the process to ensure that a proper structure is built.

Words Can Be Captivating

Some words can immediately command our attention. I recently read a book that devoted a whole chapter to the word *broken*. At first, I thought about the word and its meaning to me, and a number of impressions immediately struck me—that of a family torn by the loss of a beloved member, that of a young man robbed of his youth by years of incarceration, that of an elderly adult stricken with degenerative effects of a devastating disease or a character in a novel who had been emotionally damaged by a traumatic life experience. Not in my wildest dreams could I have envisioned me as the one who was broken.

For instance, when I hear the word *justice*, I generally pause, even if only for a moment, to listen and hear what comes next. My story about justice is that which is "just" is not limited to that which is legal. Laws are needed to maintain order and civility. But justice has a moral component that extends well beyond legal dictates. Though theoretically, all members of a discrete society are subject to the same laws, rarely are laws executed equitably. Constant—same treatment and same law. Variable—unfair treatment and unfair laws. Some by intentional design (voting rights and tax loopholes) or unintended consequences (tax loopholes and voting rights) or deliberate bias. Honorable or malicious intent. Laws often raise complex issues of equality and fairness as well as justice. My personal story is that social justice involves taking care of the poor and oppressed through an equitable (not necessarily equal) distribution of wealth, opportunities, and privileges. (And Justice happens to be my father's first name and my son's middle name).

So "justice" is one of those issues that immediately captures my interest. Once I've heard exactly what is being discussed about "justice," I quickly make a judgment as to whether the conversation is worthy of my continued attention. If the conversation is about a perceived legal, moral, political, or social injustice, I'm in. If it's about a perceived indiscretion committed by someone's husband, wife, friend, or associate, I'm definitely out. The more personal it gets, the further out I go. (That is, I will never touch stuff like spousal indiscretion, even if loosely related to justice, equity, fairness, or righteousness. My neighbor did that once, and he ended up married to his best friend's ex-wife. Then he spent the rest of his life wishing he still had his friend instead of the ex-wife. Sorry, it's a long story.)

Words Can Be Confusing

There is currently an ongoing debate in the US over the need for enhanced "border security" on the US's southern border with

Mexico. One party is locked in to the perspective that the solution to border security is "a wall" across the southern border. The other party believes that the solution is more along the lines of "virtual" border security: using technological solutions such as artificial intelligence, radar sensors, and cameras. Unfortunately, "the wall" has both an explicit meaning but implicit significance.

The discussion of the "the wall" has moved well beyond a physical structure. The implicit significance has become much more important than the standard meaning. Implicitly "the wall" means a fulfilled campaign promise, a political victory, and a stance against immigration. To the opposition group, the technological solution means a political victory, a check against a perceived administrative power grab, and a shift in political priorities. These two perspectives on "border security" are a long way from a "wall" versus "technology." This just reinforces the idea that *words have significance beyond their surface meaning.*

How can you know if you and another person are operating on different understandings of certain words? The answer is, *ask!* Then *listen*—listen to yourself (reflection), listen to others (curiosity), seek to understand others (empathy), seek to learn from others (awareness), and seek closure (shared understanding). (Note that shared understanding isn't necessarily the same as agreement. You can have understanding without agreement.)

Listening is a highly underrated skill. As is characteristic of most differences of opinion, we often listen to disprove rather than understand (certainly not any stroke of wisdom on my part, but that of Steven Covey). There is often a greater *desire to "win an argument" than "understand differences."* If you can listen to another perspective and suspend your personal bias toward the righteousness of your own, a whole new world of awareness can open up to you.

Asking and listening are generally not the first response. The more probable response would be—you guessed it—give the answer rather than ask the question. This simple inquiry contains the key to reconciling most differences. What do you mean? you may ask. Well, let me tell you. Asking a question about someone else's perspective does several things:

- It heightens external *awareness* by muting internal noise. (Let me pause so I can focus on what you're saying rather than what I'm thinking.)
- It gives the other person the power of your *attention*. (I'm sincerely interested in what you have to say.)
- It encourages *defining versus defending* an opposing perspective. (What evidence do you have that causes you to believe what you believe?)
- It allows someone to more readily *empathize* with another's perspective. (I can understand why you feel that way about that?)
- It begins the process of *reconciling* the fundamental differences of each perspective. (Help me to understand what you mean by exceptional.)

Word can be inspiring ...

"But words are things, and a small drop of ink, falling like dew, upon a thought, produces that which makes thousands, perhaps millions, think." This eloquent and timeless statement written by the British poet and Romanticist Lord George Byron emphasizes the simplicity of words and the nurturing impact they have on contemplative thought—"a small drop of ink, falling like dew, upon a thought." It also shows the magnitude of their expansive power to make "thousands" (on second thought), "perhaps millions," do something they might not otherwise have done—and that's "think." *Thinking is the engine that activates our imagination and allows us to see different things or to see things differently.*

"Words are singularly the most powerful force available to humanity. We can choose to use this force constructively with words of encouragement, or destructively using words of despair. Words have energy and power with the ability to help, to heal, to hinder, to hurt, to harm, to humiliate and to humble" (Yehuda Berg).

Implicit in Yehuda Berg's quote is the idea that words are an incredible force—"singularly the most powerful force available to humanity." Words have the power to start wars or to broker peace. They can build others up or tear them down. They have the power to do good or foster evil.

Words do indeed matter. This is obviously a cautionary warning to watch what you say because words have consequences. The same words uttered to different ears can have dramatically different effects.

Section 6: Words: The Tools of Expression

❖ Words
  ➢ Have explicit definitions
  ➢ Can have an implicit meaning (that differs from the definition)
  ➢ Context can change their meaning

❖ Word arrangements
  ➢ Building blocks of communication
  ➢ Simple structures: subject and predicate
  ➢ Complex impact: deception, division, inspiration…

❖ Word Usage
  ➢ Sender's intent
  ➢ Receiver's understanding
  ➢ Unintended consequences
  ➢ Willful distortion

❖ Communication
  ➢ "Agreement" is usually the end of inquiry.
  ➢ "Agreement" doesn't necessarily mean you agree.
  ➢ To avoid misunderstandings: ask, then listen!

VII. Thoughts: The Inspiration for Creation

Stories are reimagined experiences that are initially felt and perhaps subsequently expressed in a way that causes you and others to reasonably recreate them in your mind's eye. The experience is made more real by the choice of details shared and the intensity of emotions felt.

I'm a "Gestalty." Gestalty is, of course, not a real thing. It's just my shorthand for a follower of the Gestalt approach to psychotherapy developed by Friedrich (Fritz) Perls and his wife, Laura. The work of Fritz Perls formed the foundation for the work of other notable Gestalt psychologist and therapists, including Ralph Hefferline, Paul Goodman, Erving Polster, and Joseph Zinker. Zinker used the work of all these therapists to create a diagram of an individual's creative process as a cycle of experience. The cycle of experience took years of research to develop. Zinker used the "figure-ground" and "contact" concept to describe the cycle of experience. The cycle of experience has seven components: sensation, awareness, energy, action, contact, withdrawal, and satisfaction. *Sensation* is where the individual experiences something (the "figure") that disturbs their equilibrium. If the sensation is strong enough to hold the individual's attention, *awareness* of a need to interpret the sensation emerges. Awareness of a specific need that is seeking resolution mobilizes *energy*. The energy is released in the form of *action*, and *contact* is made with that which will satisfy the need. During contact, the environment is explored to find whatever is new or different. When the new or different element of the environment has been satisfactorily identified, destructured, and assimilated, change within the individual occurs. *Withdrawal* occurs once the original need has been satisfied. The individual then returns to a steady state and the cycle is closed. When the cycle has been completed, the individual would return to the beginning and wait for a new figure to emerge. This helped therapists conceptualize the internal process(es) that individuals go through when trying to resolve a specific need ("figure") and the things that prevent them from reaching *satisfaction*. The cycle of experience was subsequently expanded for application in group development. So what? you may ask.

I have an important disclaimer to share about what follows. As I said previously, I'm a Gestalty. I had the honor of participating in classes and discussions led by the late Edwin Nevis, the cofounder of the Gestalt Institute of Cleveland and founder of the Gestalt International Study Center. I've participated in the International Organization and Systems Development Program and studied under the able tutelage of my Gestalt friends and mentors Mary Ann Rainey and Jonno Hanafin. So I would say that though I'm not a Gestalt expert, I am conversant in and have a working knowledge of the Gestalt organization development methodology. Consequently, given my knowledge of Gestalt, limited though it may be, I can't say that it didn't influence my thinking in creating what follows.

With the help of other noted therapists, it took Zinker years to develop the "cycle of experience" consulting tool. It is supported by volumes of collective scientific research and validation. Whereas, what I've created was done on a napkin one afternoon at my favorite lunch spot (I still have the napkin with grease stains and all from the cheese fries). So any resemblance to Gestalt language or methods is purely accidental. What I've created is more art than science. However, that being said, you may still be able to find some hidden Perls in what I've done. (Did you see what I did there? I replaced pearls with Perls, as in Fritz Perls. Wasn't that clever? Never mind.)

> In the beginning
> Words were without meaning,
> Thoughts without form,
> Concepts without coherence,
> Then stories were born.

My model is called the "BS Builder," or BSB for short. It has three phases that loosely correlate to really nothing that I'm aware of.

It was purely a "figment" of my imagination. The three phases of BSB are inspiration, assimilation, and integration. The first phase, inspiration, is "imagining" or forming a mental image of something (e.g., I think I'll write a book about how biases affect the thoughts we have and the stories we create). Phase two, assimilation, is gathering the component parts needed to create what was imagined (e.g., what are some examples of biased stories and what characteristics do they share?). The integration phase is about fitting the component parts together into a meaningful and functional whole that is compatible with the environment for which it was created (e.g., how does the knowledge of biased stories affect its targeted audience and accomplish its intended purpose?).

These three phases take different forms depending on whether they are a part of an analytic process or creative process. We know that an analytic process is the act of converging "facts, data, information, judgment, experience, and wisdom" to create an outcome. Conversely, a creative process is the act of "diverging one's thinking to explore many different options."

Stories have a uniquely varied lifeline and lifespan; they're born, they're nurtured, they grow, they mature, and they expire. Some die suddenly under the burden of proof, and others live in perpetuity despite the absence of truth. Some live rich, visible vibrant lives while others live quietly in the recesses of our minds. You may be thinking, "They're just stories. Why are you treating them as though they were anthropomorphist?" (Don't ask, too many syllables for me to pronounce. But I think it means giving human characteristic to nonhuman things.) Well, if you thought that, you would be right. To me stories do have humanlike qualities. Though they are not in and of themselves organic, thinking and feeling things, they do reflect someone else's expressions of human characteristics. As such, they have the ability to activate human emotions: joy, sadness, hate, fear, anger, confusion, etc. I would think that most would agree that makes them pretty powerful.

	Inspiration	Assimilation	Integration
Analytic Process (Reason— Fact-based)	Observe Capture relevant factual data regarding a concept or theory.	Collect Methodically examine captured data.	Connect Introduce new facts that are congruent with the entire system of known facts.
Creative Process (Passion— Perception-based)	Imagine Form a mental image of an object or concept.	Transform Make the image or concept more concrete.	Create Bring into existence a new idea, image or concept.

Inspiration

Stories begin as simple ideas. These ideas can materialize by reflecting on something that happened in the past, reacting to something that is happening in the present, projecting something that may happen in the future, or imagining something that has no possibility of ever happening at all. These ideas, through the power of focus and imagination, eventually morph into recognizable images that ultimately become the drivers of creation.

The two areas that I believe are major contributors to the inspiration phase of story development are visualization and imagination. Visualization is where something that may not be immediately obvious (e.g., an experience, a feeling, a sensation, or an observation) is captured by your subconscious only to later become the focus of your considered thought. This thought might come to you out of nowhere when you least expect it. This can be any one of the unlimited sensations that you are exposed to daily but go unnoticed.

Imagination is the visual construct of a thought or idea in your mind's eye. It involves taking whatever the thing was that inspired you and mulling it over in your mind until an image emerges that resonates with your original thought. The idea may take the form of an abstract (e.g., a concept, judgment, belief) or concrete mental image (e.g., object, event, scene, conscious/subconscious).

My mother undoubtedly makes the world's best German chocolate cake (no BS, just fact). Unfortunately, I didn't inherent the baking gene. But fortunately, my brother and his daughters did. So hopefully, the recipe will live on for at least two more generations. Anyway, this is how visualization and imagination work during the visualization phase. Inspiration—I have a taste for some German chocolate cake (awareness). (Where did that come from? Maybe my chocolate "fetish" just arbitrarily kicked in. Or I was standing downwind of the local bakery midday. Or it's close to my birthday and Mom usually sends me a German chocolate cake. The truth is, I don't have a clue where that sensation came from.) Imagination—I think I should make a German chocolate cake. (I can almost see my mother's beautiful German chocolate cake, with multiple moist chocolate brown layers topped with sweet coconut pecan frosting.)

The world is full of sensations, some that we are aware of, and others that we're not. However, the sensations that we pay attention to are only those that are of personal interest to us. Sensations are the seeds from which we extract facts. Those facts are the things that stimulate us to think. How and what we think about have been the subject of scientific and academic curiosity since forever.

The Austrian psychologist Sigmund Freud created a three-tiered model of the mind: the conscious, the preconscious, and the unconscious mind. According to Freud, the conscious mind communicates with the outside world *and* our inner selves through speech, pictures, writing, and thought and represent about 10 percent of the brain's capacity. The preconscious mind can be thought of as a repository for recent memories and represents about 50–60 percent of the brain's capabilities. The unconscious mind serves as a storehouse of all memories and past experiences, both those repressed or those consciously forgotten because they no longer serve a purpose. The unconscious mind occupies the other 30–40 percent of the brain. For the sake of this discussion, the preconscious and unconscious minds will be referenced as a single entity under the umbrella term "subconscious." So "conscious" will refer to that portion of the mind used to engage the outside world and "subconscious" the part that internally organizes and recalls past memories and experiences. These subconscious memories and experiences form the basis from which our beliefs and behaviors are developed.

The subconscious mind is always available to the conscious mind. Though it may not always be fully aware, it is always mindful and impactful. It provides *meaning* for all our interactions with the outside world. It serves as a *filter* for our beliefs and habits. It communicates with our conscious mind through feelings, emotions, imagination, and sensations. Our subconscious can be influenced by our environmental surroundings even when our conscious mind isn't totally focused, such as when we're asleep or day dreaming. (Like when you've driven to a destination and then have no memory of the trip.) In these situations, our subconscious stays aware and allows us to perform as necessary.

The role of the subconscious, apart from short term memory, is to ensure that you have everything you need for quick recall in order to function effectively. They're not a continual focus, but they are there when you need them.

- Memories—your telephone number, how to drive a car, how to get home, what you need to get on the way home, etc.
- Patterns—behaviors, habits, and mood.
- Filters—beliefs and values used to test the validity of information according to your view of the world.
- Sensations—environmental information taken in through your senses and its meaning to you.

If it doesn't happen to have a filter or reference point for some bits of information that you receive, then it has a direct line to the storage place of the mind—the unconscious. It will ask the unconscious to pull out the programs that it best associates with the incoming data to help make sense of it all.

The subconscious is constantly at work. According to the NLP (neuro-linguistic programming) communication model we are assaulted with over 2 million bits of data every *second*! I don't know how accurate that number is, but let's say the number was 200 per second instead. Still a lot? Well, let's try 20 per second. That would be 1,200 per minute, 72,000 per hour and 1,728,000 per day. Just think about what would happen if your conscious mind had to deal with all that information. You would undoubtedly blow a mental fuse. (I personally top out at 10 a day.) But instead of your conscious mind having to deal with all that information, your subconscious mind handles it. It filters out all the unnecessary information and delivers to the conscious mind only what it needs at the time. It does all this behind the scenes stuff so you can perform your daily work uninhibited. And it does this as logically as it can, based on the programs it has access to in your unconscious. It then communicates all the results into consciousness via emotions, feelings, sensations, reflexes, images, and dreams—*but not words*.

Stories evolve from the sensations that stimulate our imagination. Imagination involves the ability of the mind to expand old thoughts and create new ones. It is the engine of creativity. It allows us to see ships in inkblots, dragons in clouds, and faces in rocks (even those that are not Mount Rushmore). Visualization is the process of imagining what an idea might look like if it were fully developed.

Our imagination can be both expansive and restrictive. Imaginative people can see possibilities in everything they observe. Whereas less imaginative people are easily blinded by personal thoughts and beliefs that can inhibit their ability to see possibilities. That idea can reveal itself as an impression, an uncertain thought, an unclear memory, a curious feeling, an undefined object, an unanswered question, an unresolved problem, or an imagined outcome.

I love watching TV shows that involve real or fictionalized forensic science investigations where someone is called to a crime scene and has to identify factors that allow them to determine who the perpetrator of the crime was. In most cases, especially in the made up TV dramas, what the forensic scientist (or superhero star detective) sees is not obvious to the TV audience. (If it were, then the show would be over in ten minutes instead of the usual sixty.) What they seemingly have is the superhuman ability to look at the situation, and from all the component parts of the scene, identify those that are relevant, organize them, determine their relationship, and come to a heroic "Sherlock Holmes-ish" kind of conclusion.

What these fictional characters supposedly have is a superheightened environmental sensitivity; they're able to use their senses to scan everything in the environment, retain those things that are relevant in their subconscious, and discard those that are not. They are then able to consciously organize the relevant factors in a way that is meaningful to their case.

In life, we are all junior forensic scientist in training. As stated previously, we are bombarded daily with an unimaginable amount of sensations (forensic evidence). So much so that it's impossible for us to take it all in. So obviously we don't. What we do, either consciously or subconsciously, is selectively choose certain aspects of our environment to give attention.

Sensations are feelings (heart), perceptions (mind), or contacts (body) that cause reactions of interest or excitement. They are a form of "arousal," if you will. (Okay, keep your mind out of the gutter. It's probably not what you're thinking.) The "arousal" I'm talking about is more along the lines of a stimulus response. You know, like a "stimulus package," where there is an infusion of money (stimulus) that energizes the economy (response). The economy is then stimulated to arousal. (Is that what you were thinking? If so, we're on the same page. Now where was I?)

Try the following sensory exercise: I'm an avid walker. The small community in which I live covers an area of approximately ten square miles. I've not only walked to the far reaches of every corner of my community, I've also done the same in many of the adjoining neighborhoods in other communities. No matter which direction I walk, there is something—a park that is particularly pleasant to walk through, a church that is architecturally unique, a home that has an interesting design, a neighborhood that has a wealth of mature trees—that immediately comes to mind. I walk in anticipation of seeing those landmarks. Since I've walked these streets many, many times before, I often walk "unconsciously aware" of my surroundings until I reach certain points of interest. I'm so familiar with the path I've taken that I don't consciously perceive all the sensations that I'm experiencing. When I am consciously aware, like the forensic scientist, I have a heightened sensitivity to my environment. I see the brightness of the sun, the blueness of the sky, and the greenness of the lawns. I hear the sounds of the traffic and the rumblings of a distant train. I smell the scent of the flowers or of freshly cut grass.

But believe it or not, your subconscious mind has a much stronger sense of awareness of your surroundings than your conscious mind. "How can that be?" you may ask. Well, the subconscious mind is always switched on, even when you're sleeping. So as you're being hit by all these sensations, your conscious mind may be in a semirest state, while your subconscience continues to churn. Consequently, it captures much more than the conscious mind is able to process.

As discussed previously, the beginning of most stories are rather obscure. As in the case of forensic science, they may begin as a simple external sensation (e.g., the sound of music, the color of a leaf, the smell of a spice) that captures your interest and becomes the object of considered thought. Or they may emanate from a quiet moment of meditation in which a thought (origins unknown) pops into your head and once again arouses your interest. Regardless of origin, conscious thought focuses your awareness. It is no longer an inconspicuous leaf lying unnoticed on the ground. It becomes a beautifully transformed fallen red appendage of a magnificently colored autumn oak. Thus, we have the origins of "the story of the leaf."

As the leaf example shows, if our focus on a given sensation becomes clear, we eventually move into a state of conscious "awareness." When we are aware of something it means we have conscious recognition of it. A lot of what we experience, we don't consciously realize.

If you were to walk into a new restaurant with a diverse mix of people, you would experience an unlimited number of sensations—from the sight of colorful clothing, an ornate chandelier, decorative wallpaper, and hardwood flooring, to the sounds of muted whispers, loud voices, and hardy laughter, to the smells of seasoned dishes, musky colognes, or scented perfumes. You may experience them all subconsciously but be consciously "aroused" by only a few—perhaps a particularly interesting person, an ornately framed picture, an enticingly aromatic dish or even the melding of disparate sounds.

Assimilation

Stories are the fundamental way we create meaning or make sense out of our world. They bring our thoughts to life as we take in new information and seek to understand it fully. Each story travels a unique path from inspiration to activation. Storytelling is the way we share our observations and understandings with the outside world. Our impulses to create stories are so natural and powerful that they are an automatic byproduct of each and every experience we have.

Stories are not static. They are continually growing and evolving. This evolution is at times conscious and, at other times, subconscious. Out of every experience we develop a response. That response is refined and illuminated as we engage with the environment around us. In Gestalt theory, this experience-response cycle is a basic map for how a person becomes aware of a need, mobilizes actions to meet that need, and produces some corresponding results.

Two major elements of assimilation are motivation and creation. To extend the aforementioned "Mom's cake" metaphor, motivation would sound something like, "What do I need to do?" (Where's the recipe? What are the ingredients? Semisweet chocolate, cake flour, cocoa powder, buttermilk, vanilla extract…). And creation would sound like, "Let's do it!" (Combine and mix the ingredients—in the proper order of course—heat oven to 350°F and bake for thirty to thirty-five minutes. *Voila!* The cake has arrived.)

Motivation is the process of moving an idea forward. Some ideas we act on immediately, and others we archive for later reference. We consciously or subconsciously recall select thoughts to make decisions, draw conclusions, or take actions. Unlike the subconscious mind, the conscious mind has the ability to direct our focus and arouse our imagination. Focus and imagination allow us to consciously create narratives that we feel best reflect the ideas or thoughts that we've stored. If not consciously expressed, a partial memory or impression is always retained in our subconscious. Motivation takes the ideas that we've captured and feeds them like oxygen does a flame; the more oxygen it's given, the more intense the flame. Soon the ideas become less fleeting and take a more dominant place in your psyche; it moves from an interesting idea to be pondered, to an active thing to be addressed.

Ideas may be fleeting or alluring. Fleeting ideas, such as an unusual scent or an unfamiliar sound, are more momentary; they may capture our attention for a short time, but the energy isn't sustainable. These ideas may quickly be relegated to our subconscious, never to be seen again. However, alluring ideas are more interesting or attractive to us causing us to give them conscious attention.

I really like looking at dual optical illusions: pictures where multiple figures can be seen in a single image. Most of us have seen the illusion first published in 1915 by cartoonist W.E. Hill that shows an integrated image of an old woman and a young woman. Depending on how you look at it, you may see either one or the other but not both simultaneously. That's why listening to stories is so fascinating to me. Just like the multiple figures that can be present in a single image, many facts can be present in any story. When we listen to these stories, just like with the dual images, we often see certain facts and are unable or unwilling to see others. We obviously build our understanding around the facts that we see. Generally, once we've developed a story about something, it's difficult to change it. Just as it's difficult to see the old lady once we've seen the young lady. Without having the facts (the original image) to refer to, we must rely on our memory to recreate what we saw. And our memory only records what we believe—not what we are absolutely certain we saw—either the old or the young woman, but not both.

Think about what would happen if the two people who previously viewed the hill image had to agree on what they saw. I'm sure that each would be willing to argue to the death that their version of the image, either the old woman or the young woman, was unequivocally correct and the other absolutely wrong! Without revisiting the original image (facts), their "story" about what they saw is the only thing they have to go on. Neither is wrong. Both are supported by the facts. However, each perspective is limited by the facts that were chosen. It's easy to see how competing stories can lead to conflict. Each of the variant stories is created from the facts that each person believes to be true. Each holds on to the rightness of their perspective without acknowledging the potential rightness of the other.

"Convergence" is where all facts are checked against prevailing stories. Using the dual image example, convergence may look something like the two people with the divergent perspectives getting together to view the original image (the facts). Each would then have an opportunity to explain what they saw (the facts behind their story) while viewing the image together (e.g., "The nose of the older woman appears to be the chin and cheek of the younger woman"). In this way, each would have the opportunity to see the other's perspective.

Convergence is necessary for reconciliation and validation. Reconciliation is about both parties being presented with all the facts and given the opportunity to reconcile differences. Validation is the process of ensuring that all the facts continue to support your story, and if not, using the new understanding of all the facts to create a new story.

> Convergence is often the part of reconciling differences that is skipped. Why, you might ask? Well, to put it simply, convergence is a conscious endeavor. It requires you to do something that doesn't necessarily come naturally. As Dr. Haidt pointed out we are natural story processors. We are less proficient at logic processing. We can and do create stories without a lot of reasoning. The reasoning generally comes after the story has already been created, and usually for the purpose of justifying rather than validating the story. Convergence is about validating stories. It takes all of the facts into consideration. It involves identifying the facts, verifying them (to the extent possible) and analyzing the degree

to which they support or refute the prevailing stories. The reason why convergence is usually skipped is because it takes time, energy, rigor, focus and, most importantly, openness.

The subconscious is only aroused when summoned by conscious thought. That's why if all you do is focus on "negative" things, then your subconscious will obediently deliver "negative" feelings, emotions, and memories that you have associated with that type of thinking. Those feelings can become your reality, and you can get caught up in a never-ending loop of negativity, fear, and anxiety, looking for the negative in every situation. The same is true for those who direct their thoughts toward the positive in every situation. It really depends on the type of programming your subconscious has experienced during your life. Have you been programmed to lean toward pessimism or optimism, negative thinking or positive thinking, happiness or anger, or anywhere in between? Identifying which way you sway is the beginning of improving which way you sway. The ability of your conscious mind to direct your attention and awareness is one of the most important powers we can have to change our life story. We can and should learn to control what we consciously focus on.

The other important ability of the conscious mind is visualization. Your mind can literally imagine things that are totally new and unique, something you've never experienced before. This is something your subconscious mind can't do. The subconscious can only offer limited variations of memories it has stored in your repository of past experiences. And check this out, the subconscious can't distinguish between what the conscious mind imagines and what is actually real. Whatever is brought up by conscious imagination and intently focused on, simultaneously brings up all the emotions and feelings that are associated with that image in your mind. Amazing!

What we attempt to create is often quite different from what currently exists. Outcomes are often unclear when we begin. This necessitates a period of trial and error and numerous course corrections as you discover where you want to go and how to get there.

Psychological and cultural dynamics increase its messiness, often requires a shift in mindset, behavior, and even culture to redirect. Creation of order out of chaos and the eventual return to randomness; constantly taking in new and uncharted experiences (which is the essence of chaos). There is a constant interplay of chaos and order. We experience life through the synthesis of new information through the filters and order of what we already believe. It is the brain's ability to process chaos by being open to randomness that allows us to manage all the information we are bombarded with daily. It is the capacity of the brain to filter new experiences through the existing order to generate new and ongoing illusion of experience on an ongoing basis—a fusion of order and chaos. New experiences don't rewrite the established play or established neurological mapping order. By operating in a balanced way between order and chaos, the brain integrates new information with its already stored order (*The Theater of the Brain*, Robert Berezin, MD).

Creation represents the articulation of the conclusions that we draw. It's the narrative that best reflects the mental image, the thought, belief, object, or fact that was first imagined.

- We create stories organically from some "sensation" (e.g., an experience, an observation, a conversation, a thought or a feeling).
- Stories are a product of both reality (facts) and imagination (interpretations).
- Divergent stories can be created from the same set of facts.
- Convergent evidence provides greater insights into divergent stories

When I was young, there were certain words that my parents wouldn't let me use. These weren't really the kind of bad words that have become commonplace in today's hip-hop culture and teen vernacular. I'm sure you know the words that I'm talking about—they're often referred to as four-letter words. When I was growing up, these words were never even thought of, let alone used in everyday conversation. However, there were certain words that were taboo in my parents' household, such as calling someone a liar, idiot, jerk, or arse (British for ass). These are, of course, mild by today's standards.

Since we couldn't use these words, we had to come up with other ways of expressing the thought without using the actual word. For instance, if we wanted to say that someone was telling a lie, we would say that they were telling a "story." That would be a subtle way of passing my parents' civility test.

Later in life, I realized that a "lie" really was a "story." It's a biased story that can be either a complete fabrication or a statement of fact. You may be wondering, if it's "a statement of fact," how can it be a lie? That's completely counterintuitive. Doesn't the use of facts automatically make a statement true?

Absolutely not! Statements are usually, to varying degrees, a combination of fact and fiction. Sometimes facts are the focus, and at other times, it's pure fiction. Fiction by definition is something made up, a product of our imagination. Facts can be connected with blatantly false, highly questionable, or completely disconnected statements that make the entire statement fictitious.

An example of a fact-based statement may be, "Scientific research shows that in October 1999, an iceberg the size of London broke free from the Antarctic ice shelf." For the sake of discussion, regardless of your position on global warming, let's assume that the preceding statement is a mutually acceptable "fact." Then given this fact,

- a blatantly false statement might be, "There was no depletion of the Antarctic ice shelf in the twentieth century";
- a highly questionable statement may be, "The seismic activity affecting the Antarctic ice shelf in October 1999 was insignificant"; and
- a disconnected conclusion may be, "This winter will be one of the coldest in history preventing further depletion of the ice shelf."

This gives us a lot of latitude in how we choose to tell any story, regardless of the facts. So facts combined with unfounded conjecture yields fiction.

Since stories are a combination of facts and biases, the thing that determines whether a particular assertion is true is based on our predisposed reliance on facts or personal perceptions.

- Was the story based on personal belief? (Reacting, e.g., "Guns don't kill people. People kill people.")
- Was data chosen that supported a preexisting story? (Rationalizing, e.g., "Every day ninety-three people die from gun violence. Gun violence is a mental health issue.")
- Was the story created based on facts? (Reasoning, e.g., "Every day ninety-three people die from gun violence: thirty-two are murdered, and fifty-eight kill themselves.")
- Does the story contain a coherent set of thoughts? (Reconciling, e.g., "Every day ninety-three people die from gun violence, disproportionately affecting black communities, women, and other marginalized groups.")

The first two begin with a preexisting story. The story may or may not be true. But in the "absence of data," there is a greater risk of the story being untrue (not based in fact or reality). The third gets closest to the "truth" because it begins with data. But it can also be untrue.

*****

1. Did you create your story from your experience? Was the story created based on the experience of others?
   (Reacting) "personal beliefs" are the data. An action performed or a feeling experienced in response to a situation or event.
2. Did you create your story based on what you believe and then choose data to support the story you created?
   (Rationalizing) "personal beliefs" are the basis for choosing data. Attempt to explain or justify (one's own or another's behavior or attitude) with logical, plausible reasons, even if these are not true or appropriate.

3. Did the story you created come from the data you gathered? (Reasoning) data is the basis for establishing belief. The action of thinking about something in a logical, sensible way.

4. Is your story made up of a coherent set of compatible thoughts?
   (Reconciling) the act of ensuring that one thought or belief is closely related or compatible with another.

The first is a belief, a hunch, a guess with a biased choice of facts to support it. The second is a prediction, a hunch, a guess, but with a reference to some historical data that may support it. The third comes the closest to the "truth" because it is purely fact-based. The fourth links the concept of gun violence with its impact on marginalized populations. The story may or may not be true. But facts don't necessarily guarantee that a statement is true. But in the "absence of data," there is a greater risk of the story lacking credibility (not based in fact or reality).

Integration

Chaos theory states that within the apparent randomness of complex chaotic systems, there are underlying patterns of order that emerge. Chaos theory is often referenced in discussions on change. I was once told that no meaningful change occurs without going through a period of chaos. In the middle of change, processes can be messy and outcomes uncertain. But ultimately, out of chaos comes order—some level of standardization, certainty, and predictability. This stable postchaotic state is similar to what I call story integration, the phase of story creation where it reaches reasonable completion or satisfactory closure.

Creating a story is obviously only half "the story." Stories are created for a purpose; to entertain, to explain, to educate, to influence, etc. However, the real significance of a story is the impact it has on our thoughts and behaviors as well as those of others. There can be a huge gap between a story's intent and its ultimate impact.

A couple of questions that might deepen our understanding of a story's impact are "Is the story's message clear, concise, and unambiguous? Does the story communicate its message in a way that accomplishes its intended purpose?"

Integration is the process of ensuring that the story successfully fulfills its intended purpose. The outcome of integration is the confirmation (or refutation) that your story has indeed had the cogent impact that you had hoped for. Integration is the melding of stories into our conscious understanding or subconscious memory for future use. Its ultimate goal is to maintain, protect, and sustain a story's long-term existence.

Two important elements of integration are normalization and preservation. A story is normalized when it becomes commonplace in our thinking. Normalized stories are those that have successfully fulfilled their intended purpose and settled into a permanent resting place in our psyche. Story preservation is when a story finds a resting place not only in your psyche but also in the psyche of others preserved for posterity. These stories have some special meaning that causes us to value and appreciate them for weeks, months, years, decades, and even centuries after they are first shared.

Who once wrote, "I've learned that people will forget what you said, people will forget what you did, but people will never forget how you made them feel." Now that's story integration at its finest. (I know, it's my BS.)

BS Section 7: Thoughts—The Inspiration for Creation

❖ Inspiration—to pay attention.
  ➢ thoughts that are fed by imagination are the engine of creativity.
  ➢ Sensations—information taken in through our senses.
  ➢ Sigmund Freud's three-tiered model of the mind.
    o Conscious mind—uses other parts of the mind to interact with the outside world.
    o Preconscious mind—storage area for recent memories.

      o   Unconscious mind—storage for all memories and past experiences.

❖ Assimilation—to form an idea.
- ➤ What begins as a sensation can become the object of considered thought.
- ➤ Conscious—subconscious role in story creation.
  - o The *subconscious* is only aroused when summoned by the conscious mind.
  - o *Conscious awareness* is the process of forming a mental image;
  - o *Conscious bias* is being aware of the feelings, emotions and memories that cause you to react to a sensation.
  - o *Unconscious bias* is being unaware of the sub-conscience "call" that occurs when you experience an event.
- ➤ Determine the purpose; to entertain, to explain, to educate, to influence, etc.
- ➤ Selecting both relevant facts and reasoned interpretations that you feel will support the story you created.
- ➤ Develop a preliminary "storyboard" of thoughts and ideas that support the story's intent.

❖ Integration—to bring into existence; translating from abstract to concrete.
- ➤ "Words are singularly the most powerful force available to humanity…"(Yehuda Berg).
- ➤ Key elements of story creation include purpose, content and structure.
- ➤ Integration is the culmination of a story's creation.
- ➤ A story's significance is its sustainable impact on our thoughts and behaviors.
- ➤ Ultimate choice to strengthen, renew, and reinforce or subdue, repress, and discard.

VIII. The Tale the Hearer Heard

Whenever we hear a story, we hear it through the filter of our past experiences. This automatically activates parts of our brain that make linkages to the ideas, thoughts and emotions that were previously experienced. Consequently, some experience certain stories more intimately than others.

D istinguished journalist, author and historian Jon Ellis Meacham once said "The American revolution was about reason—the fact that we would actually think about things with our minds instead of reacting with our guts. That's a lot of what the enlightenment values were about in the 18th century and right now we are deferring to our passions instead of employing our reason. Hoping that these hearings and what today does is shed light rather than just generate heat." The world is full of shallow thinkers who rely more on their gut than reasoned thought. I don't know whether it's because they are incapable of or too lazy to explore all sides of an issue in pursuit of true understanding.

I recently heard a discussion about healthcare in America where two opposing perspectives were being heatedly argued. One party touted the "exceptionalism" of the American healthcare system and challenged his opponent to name another country in the world that more people go to for treatment of unusual or extreme medical conditions.

His opponent responded, "Yes, the US has some of the best specialist in the world regardless of medical discipline. However, in terms of efficiency, access, cost, and life expectancy, the US ranks at or near the bottom compared to other developed nations." Who's right? *(Selective choice of facts.)*

Well, in this particular case, it's hard to determine who's "right" and who's "wrong." Nonetheless, you as the reader have probably already determined who you believe has the "rightest" perspective.

It's just what we do *(we get to choose)*. However, both arguments can be compelling depending on the perspective of the listener. If you believe that our physician expertise and medical technology are the things that make us exceptional, you may agree with the first perspective. However, if you believe healthcare access, cost, and efficiency are the basis for an exceptional healthcare system, you may lean more toward the second. Rationalization is just the process of justifying what you already believe. We usually rationalize by "cherry-picking" all the facts that support what we already believe. Again, not unusual, just what we do.

Politicians create this conundrum all the time. They speak of America in hyperbolic terms. Anyone who declares that America is less than "exceptional" in any context runs the risk of being labeled anti-American or unpatriotic. If we both agree on American "exceptionalism," why isn't that the end of the discussion? Because if we agree at this level, it doesn't necessarily mean that we are in full agreement. (What?) It means that we agree superficially based on our understanding of how the word in question is defined. We may agree that America has an "exceptional" healthcare system but not realize that while we agree with the general assertion, it may be for very different reasons. Unfortunately, *agreement often leads to the end of inquiry.* If we were to inquire beyond any superficial agreement, we may realize that our reasons for "agreement" are vastly different. And in fact, we really don't agree at all.

Given the interpretive nature and inherent bias of stories, people respond to them in many different ways. "If we listen to a PowerPoint presentation with boring bullet points, certain parts of the brain get activated. Scientists call these Broca's area and Wernicke's area [areas of the brain that control language development and speech comprehension]. Overall, it hits our language processing parts of the brain, where we decode words into meaning. If someone tells us about how delicious certain foods were, our sensory cortex lights up. If it's about motion, our motor cortex [which coordinates the body's movements] gets activated."

When we are told a story, all areas of the brain that we would use to experience the events of the story are activated. That's why even though we may take the same path, we may experience the journey quite differently. You may experience the radiance of the flowers as I experience the harshness of the cobblestone (please excuse my metaphorically poetic moment). So if you happen to like flowers, the journey may be aesthetically pleasing to you. However, if the cobblestone happens to hurt your feet, the journey will be physically displeasing to you. So if each of us was asked to describe the journey years from now, my companion may describe it as having been an extremely pleasant experience that increased their sensitivity to the beauty around them and influenced their creative juices to the point that they were motivated to begin painting the beautiful floral works of art that are now displayed and sold in galleries around the world. Whereas, I may remember it as the journey from hell and the start of my current foot and knee problems for which I wear special order—and by the way, very expensive—orthotics that make the permanent limp that I developed less pronounced. Same path, different experience (exaggerated for effect). I'm sure that I saw the flowers and my travel companion felt the cobblestone, but with *differing degrees of relevance and levels of intensity.* The flowers "popped" for her in a way that they didn't for me. Whereas the cobblestone "popped" for me in a very different way than they did for her (or she had much better shoes than I did).

So this brings me to the second half of my premise—*we find ways to rationalize, dispel, or ignore the data that doesn't support our beliefs or serve our interests.* So let's revisit our little bittersweet journey down the floral-lined cobblestone path. Let's begin with the two very different memories about the journey. If someone were to later ask each person whether they would recommend the journey, how do you think they would respond? One may describe it as inspirationally beautiful—a journey you just have to see to believe—a definite go. The other might describe it as similar to what you may imagine the road to Hades would be—painfully perilous—a journey you might want to postpone until your next life. This might cause the person asking the question to think, "Are they talking about the same journey?" It's clear to see that *both conveniently excluded certain data, even though they may have been clearly aware that it existed.*

For the person being asked to make the recommendation, their perception of the journey is more important to share than the data that drove their perception. However, with the two perspectives being so radically different, the receiver's head is probably rotating around in circles like Linda Blair in the 1973 movie *The Exorcist*. They're no closer to being able to make a decision about whether to take the journey than they were before. Why—because they've only received the BS—not the data they need to make an informed decision. The data needed are the *facts behind the BS*. They need to know that the thing that caused the experience to be so pleasurable for one was the presence of flowers (fact) combined with their love of flowers (value). And the thing that made it so unpleasant for the other was the cobblestone path (fact) and their desire for comfort (value).

How do you think the person asking for a recommendation would feel about the path if they usually have an immediate and extreme allergic reaction to even the thought of flowers, let alone being physically surrounded by them for hours on end? The flower thing probably wouldn't work too well for them. How about if this person annually walked the John Muir Trail in the Sierra Nevada mountains and loved the challenge of rough terrain (particularly those with cobblestone paths)? Then this might be just the trip for them.

The point is that with only the BS of both perspectives, the receiver doesn't have enough relevant data to make an informed decision. With nothing more than each person's BS, we are arguably no better informed than we were before receiving their BS, or are we?

I would argue that we probably are better despite only having BS. Why? Because *in the absence of information, we use what we already know to fill the gap*. You might have a question about what you may already know that will be relevant to a decision about a disputed journey that you know nothing about.

The answer is—absolutely nothing! We have very little "relevant" information about the journey itself. But what we do have are the experiences of the two providers of information. So now our focus may shift from relevant data to data that is probably unrelated to the decision at hand, such as, "Do I like or trust the person I'm getting the information from?" "Who was the most convincing in their delivery?" "Who was the nicest?" This is a quite natural and comfortable shift. Why? Because we're essentially shifting from someone else and what they know, back to us and what we value (from our observation and experience). How many times have you seen someone accept information from one person that they previously rejected from another? I am more willing to accept information from my wife whom I love, trust, admire, adore, and know she has my best interest at heart (at least most of the time) than I am from someone that I just met. This is purely based on the strength of our preexisting relationship and not on the validity of the information she might share. However, if the topic is technology related, my trust may (possibly, probably, almost certainly) be placed somewhere other than with my wife (sorry, babe). I would strongly consider going with a stranger's perspective, again, based on past experiences (which I choose not to share at this time for obvious reasons. Love you dear!). So *the BS that we choose to accept is often related to our relationship with the source of the BS.*

However, when data (fact) is thrown into the mix, it increases the likelihood of a person being able to make an informed decision that aligns with their wants, needs, and desires (values). The other point is that the third party "experienced" the data quite differently than even the first two did. So values are an integral part of our experience.

"We tend to be attracted to (and like) people who we know well and share similar interests. The stronger our relationship with another person, the more likely we are to believe them when they tell us something."

I'm particularly fascinated with autostereograms, where you look at a two-dimensional image that appears to be nothing more than multicolored dots. But if you adjust your eyes just right, an incredible three-dimensional scene emerges. I've seen a living room, a pyramid, a whole city, and an active underwater scene, including a school of fish, magically appear. As I mentioned before, I also like dual optical illusions where multiple figures can be seen in a single image. In the Hill image both an older woman and a younger woman can be seen. Depending on how you look at it, you will see either one or the other.

I've seen a similar image with a frog and a horse (and for the longest time, I could not see that horse). This is another example of how we often see things differently and take different things away from the same experience. Again, if you were to send two people into a room at different times to view the Hill image and discuss what they saw afterward, one might say they saw an image of a beautiful young woman, the other an image of a haggard old lady (divergent stories).

How difficult do you think it would be for each to convince the other that what they saw was the true image? And I'm sure if the disagreement went unresolved long enough, one or both might suggest the conspiratorial explanation that the pictures were switched between viewings. (In the absence of information, assumptions fill the gap.) If both of the disagreeing parties are allowed to view the image together, each explaining their perspective, I am certain both would eventually be able to see the perspective of the other (convergence). However, it might take some a little longer than others. (I still can't see that darn horse.)

Another optical illusion designed by artist Sandro del PreteWorld is titled "Message d'Amour des Dauphins." If you look at the image one way, you may see two nudes in an intimate position (I know what you may be thinking, but not that intimate). If you look at the same image in another way, you may see not one, not two, but nine dolphins. Research regarding this image showed that most young children saw the dolphins but not the intimate nude couple. While most adults immediately saw the nudes, they couldn't see the dolphins without assistance.

Now why do you think that would be true? Is it because most adults are tainted? Well, not necessarily tainted, but shall we say, more experienced in the area of intimacy (if your kids first see the nude couple, I think it might be a little late for the birds and bees conversation). Most children obviously don't have a visual image or prior memory of such an intimate experience to draw on. There is a greater probability that they have seen an image of frolicking dolphins from either their computer, video game, book, or TV. So both adults and children use references or mental images that are readily available to them; children—animals, and adults—well, enough said. An interesting point is that once you see one of the images, it becomes even more difficult to see the second. Why? Because the first image we see is committed to memory and becomes part of our cognitive experience. I need look no further. I've seen the dolphins with which I am familiar. So if I look at the picture again, I see that which I have seen before and know—the dolphins.

If someone asks, "Did you see the nude couple in the image?" possible responses might be, "Where? Show me" (scientist) or, "No. Based on what I saw, there was no nude couple" (pundit) or, "It is possible that a single image can be viewed in two different ways" (expert) or, "There was no nude couple" (ideologue) or, "Whatever you say [even though I know there were only dolphins]" (opportunist).

Responses to BS

The "intent" of a story is the purview of the storyteller. However, the "impact" of a story is strictly owned by the story's audience. Why? Because people are different; they have differing points of reference (as we saw in the previous examples of dual optical illusions). It would be nice if we all thought alike (well, on second thought, maybe not). But it would at least allow us all to get along (well, maybe not; even identical twins raised in the same environment don't always agree). The fact is that we all see the image but that image can be seen in numerous ways.

React

The purest form of response is just to "react"; not a well-thought-out, logically constructed, cohesive thought, but more a pure, unfiltered, raw, uncompromising, "devil may care," "take it or leave it" reaction. Something that bypasses the head and comes straight from the heart. The "CELEBRITY-X IS STILL

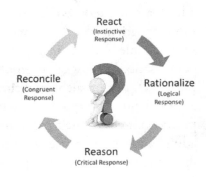

FAT!" may be an example of one of those unfiltered, spontaneous responses. It was what that person felt regardless of what anyone else thought. The celebrity being discussed was fat, and that was a fact—period!

These impulsive responses to a situation or event are without regard to fact or truth. They are stories that are created without fore-thought and are steeped in personal biases (e.g., "Guns don't kill people, people kill people").

Rationalize

Many states have laws on the books that give a person the right to defend themselves against perceived threats even to the point of lethal force. You might recognize these as stand-your-ground laws. In my opinion these laws represent an intolerable threat to public safety. They essentially sanction the escalation of violence under the ambig-uous notion of a "perceived threat." As you can imagine, most abus-ers of these laws use the defense of perceived threat to justify their actions. These are extreme examples of rationalizations; attempts to create a plausible explanation or justification for an event after the fact. In most stand-your ground cases the justifications for using deadly force are usually obvious fabrications. However, we are often guilty of more subtle forms of rationalizations in our daily lives. How about justifications for being tardy (you know, "my dog swallowed my keys") or being moody ("I didn't get much sleep last night"). Some questions that might give you insights into rationalizations are—Did the storyteller create the story first and then seek to find data to support what was created (rationalizing)? Did the storyteller attempt to explain or justify their story even though it was knowingly untrue or inappropriate (justifying)?

Reason

Reasoning is the act of thinking through something in a logi-cal, sensible, and factual way. It involves identifying and analyzing the factors that influenced your thoughts. Consequently, data plays a major role. Reasoning tackles questions such as—Did the story you created come from the data you gathered? Are there alternative perspectives to the story you created? And if so, what are the pluses and minuses of those perspectives? Having preeminent world renowned specialist in a variety of different medical disciplines is definitely a desirable thing to have. However, having a stable of highly skilled specialist that most people can't afford might be considered less than exceptional. Providing affordable healthcare services to all may also be considered a good thing. On the other hand, providing affordable healthcare that is ineffective or of poor quality would probably be less than optimal. As long as there are different understandings of what "exceptional" is, there can be no real reconciliation of differences. If one defines exceptional as "quality of service" and the other as "access to service," can there really ever be a meaningful reconciliation of differences until that's known? I would venture to say "no" because neither person understands the other's perspective. Every time the word *exceptional* enters the conversation, it conjures up a different thought for each (imagination, optical illusion).

Reconcile

The stories we create are not always logical or well thought out. Therefore, reconciliation is a logical extension of effective reasoning. Reconciliation is the process of defining the factors that influence an event then settling differences about the cause or meaning of the event. So, what do we need to move from reasoning to reconciliation? The answer is a "common image." A solution will most likely never be reached until there is a shared understanding and agreement about just what it is to be "exceptional." If exceptional means the availability of quality care then the first argument might prove to be true. If exceptional means access to low-cost healthcare for all, then the second might be true. If exceptional means access to the highest-quality medical care at an affordable price for all, then neither might be completely true. While both remain partially true.

In the aforementioned healthcare example, if one perspective is that the American system is "exceptional" and the other that it's not, there are two possible things that might happen. One, the discussion can remain at the "I'm right, you're wrong" level (then escalate into a heated argument that morphs into hurt feelings, avoidance, estrangement, subsequently depression, divorce, alimony… Sorry, I got carried away with my story. Back to what I was saying…). At the "I'm right, you're wrong" stage, both parties can self-righteously hold on to their perspective. At this point, the differences are implicit. They're not clearly defined or expressed. All we have now are competing opinions.

Being aware of and responsible for the BS we choose to consume is becoming increasingly more difficult. It is virtually impossible to discern fact from fiction. However, here are some tips from the experts on what we can do individually and collectively to navigate the BS minefields (Dr. Seargeant and Dr. Bell).

EARS Model

Empathize

Personal intuition. Listen for the story's intent beyond its obvious content. Try to read "between the lines." Be wary of any emotional reactions you might have. Though you shouldn't fully rely on your "gut," you shouldn't ignore it either. Mull it around. Make sure your gut reaction isn't just your biases clouding your view.

Source bias. Always consider the motivation of the author. Is the story intended to be a factual account or fanciful rendition of something? This is important because they require different levels of attention and standards of judgment. Be sensitive to the nature of the story. Is it singularly biased or well rounded? Also, be sensitive to the tone and tenor of the story. Relative to its purpose, does it feel sincere and heartfelt or artificial and contrived?

Analyze

Relevant facts. If *surveys* are quoted, check a survey's sample size to ensure it is statistically significant. The smaller the sample, the higher the probability of a "random aberration." Ensure survey sample is representative of the population it is intended to reflect (e.g., income level, demographic area, party affiliation), that it actually measures what it is intended to measure (e.g., "one in five British Muslims sympathized with jihadists and jihad never mentioned"), and the context or presentation isn't conducive to distortion (e.g., percentage used instead of numbers, irregular time frames used to distort averages, anomalies used instead of averages).

Source credibility. If presented as *fact*, check to determine whether the facts used come from a reputable source. Check the URL and be skeptical of news organizations you've never heard of. Check if the same facts are reported on multiple websites or broadcast networks. Verify reputable fact-checking sites (e.g., Snopes, factcheck. org, BBC's Reality Check). Make sure you know whose facts and figures are being reported. Are they from a national or international statistical office report or a survey conducted by a renowned research company or scientific institution? As we are all well aware, wild, unfounded assertions and illogical interpretations are often presented as facts. Discerning the difference has become increasingly challenging sense opinions are often presented as facts.

Factual proportionality. Proportionality generally refers to the amount of evidence needed to prove the "truthfulness" of any given assertion. An assertion is considered to be "true" if there is an "adequate" amount of evidence to support it. The amount of evidence needed to validate an assertion depends on how extraordinary the assertion is; the greater the assertion, the greater the amount of data needed to prove it.

Reflect

Personal discernment. Be aware of your perceptions and their positive and negative affect on your ability to understand and comprehend. Personal discernment is akin to critical thinking and nuanced judgement.

Thought congruence. Seek more than a surface understanding of the premises, perspectives, and feelings that underlie a story. Be aware of recurring themes, keywords, and catchphrases that may provide insight into a story's true intent. If actually presented as an opinion piece, commentary, or op-ed, ensure that the facts used are credible and the conclusion logically flows from those facts.

Select

Empirical support. Ensure that the source of the information that you choose is validated by credible observation or scientific experimentation. The information should not only be adequate enough to gain acceptance but also congruent with all other factual support.

Logical sense. Ensure that all interconnected parts of a story clearly and reasonably flow from its premises and align with it conclusions.

Emotional balance. Be aware of your personal biases in storytelling. Are you predisposed to be more receptive to scientific, expertise, punditry, opportunism, or ideologues? Analyze the limitations of your approach. Are you acknowledging only what you already knew and believed causing you to block out new information and perspectives?

Section 8: The Tale the Hearer Heard

- ❖ How stories are experienced
  - ➢ When we hear a story, all areas of the brain that we would use to experience an event are activated (Leo Widrich).
  - ➢ We experience stories with differing degrees of relevance and levels of intensity.
  - ➢ We find ways to rationalize, dispel, or ignore the data that doesn't support our beliefs or serve our interests.
  - ➢ In the absence of new information, we use what we already know to fill the gap.
  - ➢ The BS that we choose to accept is often related to our relationship with the source of the BS.

- ❖ esponses to BS
  - ➢ React—a raw and unfiltered reaction
  - ➢ Rationalize—a plausible explanation
  - ➢ Reason—logical, sensible, factual
  - ➢ Reconcile—congruent, compatible coexistence

Ears Model

- ➢ Empathize
  - o Personal intuition—story's intent beyond obvious content
  - o Source bias—motivation of the story's author
- ➢ Analyze
  - o Relevant facts—facts that are appropriate to the story's intent
  - o Source credibility—facts that originate from a reputable source
  - o Factual proportionality—adequate facts to support the validity of an assertion

- ➤ Reflect
  - o Personal discernment—awareness of personal biases and their influence on your assessment
  - o Thought congruence—more than a surface understanding of story premises and perspectives
- ➤ Select
  - o Empirical support—adequacy and congruence of factual support
  - o Logical sense—reasonability and rationality of conclusions
  - o Emotional balance—awareness of the effects of personal biases

IX. Cultural BS

Categorizing people, sorting them into groups, and ascribing a common set of traits to each group is something that we do naturally. The ascribed traits are used to differentiate one group from another. They create boundaries based on what the perceiver believes to be true or otherwise beneficial.

Philip Fernbach wrote "On our own, individuals are not well equipped to separate fact from fiction, and they never will be. Ignorance is our natural state" (wow, that hurts). A 2014 survey by Scott Neuman of NPR revealed that one in four Americans believe that the sun rotates around the earth. Those of us who believe in science know that the earth revolves around the sun. (Well, at least three quarters of us.) "Knowledge isn't in my head or in your head. It's shared. Most of what anyone knows about any topic is a placeholder for information stored elsewhere, in a long forgotten textbook or in some expert's head. Such collective delusions illustrate both the power and the deep flaw of human thinking. It is remarkable that large groups of people can coalesce around a common belief when few of them individually possess the requisite knowledge to support it." Knowing the limitations of our knowledge and capabilities "can help us differentiate the questions that merit real investigation from those that invite a reactive superficial analysis. It can also prompt us to demand expertise and nuanced analysis from our leaders which is the only tried and true way to make effective policy."

Stories can and do change over time. When I was a child, I was taught to watch, listen, and learn. I was also taught to respect the opinions of those with greater knowledge, experience, expertise, and wisdom. I don't know if others were taught these things, but for me, somewhere along the line "the script got flipped." Culturally, we seem to have moved away from seekers of scientific expertise to followers of opportunistic ideologies. Pundits have become mouthpieces for positions versus arbiters of truth. Once universally accepted words of wisdom seem to no longer apply. "Act with integrity" seems to have been superseded by "Win at all cost." What happened to all of those youthful mantras like, "It's not whether you win or lose but how you play the game," or "You're defined by how you play the game, not by the game itself" (Chuck Pagano), or "Great people have great values and great ethics" (Jeffrey Gitomer). These seem to have been overridden by "It's not how you play the game—it's how you place the blame" (Don Simpson) or "Second place is just the first-place loser" (Dale Earnhardt) or "Show me a good loser, and I'll show you a loser" (Vince Lombardi).

BS emphasis on scientific expertise

BS emphasis on opportunistic ideologies

At any given time there can be multiple levels of human-biased systems at work. Individuals, subgroups, and total group. *Individuals* are single-human entities having a unique set of personal values, beliefs, assumptions, and understandings. *Subgroups* are a collective of individuals that may be linked together by shared values, beliefs, or interests—be they social, business, religious, political, ethnic, or national affiliation. *Total group* is a broader collective of related subgroups; for example, all departments in a business (or all units sharing a similar function), all members of a particular religion (or members of that religion in a particular geographical area), all nations of the world (or nations in a particular part of the world, such as the Middle East).

The boundaries of each system can be uniquely defined (gerrymandered) based on some predetermined purpose. For instance, the boundaries for intersecting levels of *religious systems* may be congregants (individual), choir (subgroup), all church members (total group); or Christian (individual), United Methodist (subgroup), Protestant (total group); or Christian (individual), Catholic (subgroup), all Christian faiths (total group); or Muslim (individual),

Sunni Muslim (subgroup), all Muslims (total group). In each of these examples, the first dimension represents an individual religious choice. The second represents a broader subgroup designation of which the individual system is a part. And finally, the third dimension or total group reflects the totality of groups under consideration, of which the individual and subgroups systems are a subset. Obviously, the number of combinations is unlimited.

Religion can be considered one dimension of a broader scheme of cultural traits. Each culture is a collective of traits shared by a people, a nation, or other social group. So in addition to religion, cultures can be distinctively defined by various combinations of elements such as race, ethnicity, nationality, traditions, and institutions, to name a few.

The reason that this is important is that *individuals are obviously not monolithic in their thinking*. I rarely think differently than I think (yes, you did read that correctly). Consequently, I rarely have disagreements with myself (at least not anymore). But individuals not only think different things but also think about them differently. Obviously, the larger the group, the greater the potential for divergence. The more divergent the thoughts, the more difficult it becomes to reconcile differences. Therein lies the seeds of discordant BS that can lead to frustration, dissention, anger, and conflict.

Culturally Biased Stories

An elephant, a monkey, and a horse applied for a job working in a warehouse. The job title was "warehouse associate," with very little information on the duties and responsibilities of the job. Consequently, each of the applicants was pretty much left to their own understanding of what "warehouse associate" meant. The elephant prepared by loading and unloading large storage boxes on an elevated platform. The horse prepared by running several miles a day with small boxes in tow. The monkey prepared by repeatedly scampering up and down a tree to the point of exhaustion. Surely his endurance and agility would ensure that he would be the best candidate for the job.

Finally, the day of the interview arrived. The interviewer just happened to be of the monkey persuasion. The monkey, in his role as interviewer, covered the job description. After which, he explained that there would be a screening test to determine who would be most suited for the job. The interviewer began by saying, "To be fair in selection, everybody has to take an exam. We give everyone the same exam because we strive for equality and fairness in everything we do. That being said, please turn around. The test is located immediately behind you." All turned to come face-to-face with two sprawling sixty-foot white stinkwood trees. Each of the applicants looked with confusion at the massive trees, then at one another, and finally, back at the interviewer.

The interviewer, seeing the confusion on their faces, began to explain, "In order to be considered for the job, each of you must do the following. You must climb the tree on the left, follow the path denoted by the painted white arrows, jump to the adjacent tree, retrieve the red flag, reverse directions, and return to the starting line."

The monkey smiled broadly, the horse sniffled, barely able to hold back tears, and the elephant walked out in disgust, stepping on a chair and crushing it as he exited. The interviewer was completely surprised by the disparate reactions of the applicants.

- Monkey number 1 (the interviewer) felt the interviews were fair and equitable.
- Monkey number 2 (the applicant) felt the process was unexpected and fortuitous. ("I don't know what climbing a tree has to do with working in a warehouse, but it works for me. I'm golden.")
- The horse felt the process was unfair and disappointing. ("I'm the fastest in this group. I would be much more effi-

cient than the others at getting things done. I never learned tree climbing in school. This test is so unfair.")

- The elephant felt the whole thing was stupid, frustrating, and frankly, a waste of time. ("I'm the strongest of the group. If they had told me about the prescreening test in advance, I would have stayed home. I've knocked a lot of trees down in my lifetime, but climbing one, what a waste of time.")

Monkeys, horses, and elephants are all around us. Of course, in the animal kingdom, there are obvious physical differences. With humanoids, physical differences are more artificial than substantive since all humanity originated from the same seed. Commonly highlighted human differences are man-made social constructs (WEB DuBois) often used to differentiate people by either physical attributes (e.g., "black" or "white"), economic affluence (e.g., rich, poor), demographic origins (e.g., Africa or Europe), or behavioral norms (e.g., religion, politics). Our biases determine how we see these superficial differences. A "rich white Anglo-Saxon Protestant" is certainly seen as different from a "rich black Afrocentric Baptist" despite both being rich. Superficial biological differences are usually the basis for bias and culture the basis for educational, social, and economic disparities. "We see biology, we experience culture."

Let's think of monkeys, horses, and elephants as metaphors for three different cultures. Studies show that cultural differences are often the primary contributors to the gap in basic literacy and numeric skills between kids from different socioeconomic environments. "Kids from higher socioeconomic areas tend to have access to information and resources earlier and more frequently than those of lower status. So those of lower status not only begin at a deficit, but the gap in abilities tends to increase over time." This is an example of opportunity bias, where factors beyond someone's control are used to either restrict or inhibit their ability to perform.

As in the preceding story, the monkey was the beneficiary, and the horse and elephant were the unfortunate victims of opportunity bias. The system was obviously biased in the monkey's favor.

Likewise, in most cultures, there are people that are advantaged strictly based on birthrights, physical attributes, or economic status. This usually provides those fortunate enough to be born into it or otherwise acquire it, opportunities not available to others.

Cultural biases are, simply stated, biased stories (BS) about other cultures. Cultural biases cause a member of one culture to interpret or judge the values, belief, behaviors, physiology, institutions, or traditions of another culture as right, wrong, good, bad, appropriate, or inappropriate based on the standards of their own culture.

As stated previously, individuals are not monolithic in their thinking. However, individuals either self-identify or are socially organized into categorical groups (e.g., white Anglo Saxon American, African American Christian, Sunni Muslim American, Native Indian American). According to the German social psychologist Henri Tajfel, "imposing category distinctions on groups divides the social world into different groupings of people" that are judged stereotypically by others (perceivers). Perceivers exaggerate the differences in other groups to satisfy their needs or serve their purposes (e.g., "Muslims believe in peace [or Sharia]," "blacks are survivors [or prone to criminal activity]," "Asians are smart [or docile]"). These shorthand cultural descriptions reflect the perceiver's knowledge, beliefs, or assumptions about the subject group. They are nothing more than cognitive constructs that are usually created to emphasize a particular group characteristic that may or may not be true, but are often "distorted beyond reality" (Hoffman 1986). They are intended to evoke a desired response from the receiver, be it positive or negative. These descriptions are more about influencing perceptions than informing understandings.

Tajfel conducted a series of experiments related to categorization. What he found was that when people are put into groups it has a direct impact on their cognitive judgment and, correspondingly, on resulting behavior. In other words, members of a designated group will develop an identity affinity. Who would have thought that the simple act of forming a group could cause such polarization. Tajfel concluded that "imposing category distinctions (on groups) was like dividing the social world into different groups of people (e.g., French, Germans, British). The results showed how cognitively deep-seated it was for perceivers to assume that the members of different categories differed more than they did." Tajfel's findings shed so much light on the divisive nature of today's social and political environment. Once you're identified and are accepted as a member of a particular group, your priorities, judgments, and perceptions tend to consciously or subconsciously favor that group, and your loyalties are often either demanded by or biased toward that group depending on how much you value being a member.

So how we define a group's boundaries can have unintended consequences on how groups see one another. Political groups structured as they are, Democrats and Republicans, naturally pit the two groups against one another in pursuit of political power. (Note: the political primary process pits Republicans against Republicans and Democrats against Democrats in pursuit of party leadership with the opportunity to compete for the grand prize, the presidency.)

What if—just what if—we were to list the candidates without their political affiliation? What if there were five weeks of campaigning followed by one day of elections in two hundred comparably sized districts. Each district would then send a single delegate to represent the winning candidate from their district to vote for the president? What do you think would happen?

Let me guess. First, in each of the two hundred districts' groups would form to support their chosen candidate. Secondly, subsets of the two hundred divisions will join together to support an agreed upon candidate.

The following are a few cultural categories and the biases (BS), pros and cons, associated with each.

Cultural Elements

Race	Ethnicity	Nationality	Faith	Institutions	Traditions
Physiology	Culture	Origins	Values	Laws	Customs
Physiological Classification	Ethnic Affiliation	Heredity	Religious Doctrines	Social, Economic, Political Rules	Common Historical Rituals
Black, White, Yellow, Brown	American, African, European	French, German, Russian, Japanese	Muslim, Christian, Jewish, Buddhist, Hindis, Atheist	Constitution, Capitalism, Socialism, Congress	Holidays, Ceremonies, Food, Dress
Deprecative Cultural BS					
Racism – prejudice or discrimination against another race based on belief of superiority	Ethnocentrism – evaluation of other cultures as inferior and personal cultural superiority	Nationalism – support for the interest of ones nation to the detriment of another's	Islamophobia / Antisemitism – fear, hatred or prejudice toward another religion	Institutional Racism – racism expressed in the practices of social and political institutions	Xenophobia – fear or hatred of strangers, foreigners or anything that is unfamiliar
Appreciative Cultural BS					
Believing and expressing the idea that racial groups have equitable capabilities	Believing and expressing the idea that other cultures are neither inferior nor superior but different	Rejecting superiority of cultural standards and equalizing cultural differences among national groups	Understanding, respecting and affirming the non-intrusive non-injurious elements of other religions or beliefs	Expressing and supporting social and political practices that lead to institutional policies that lead to racial equity	Having racialized ideas about stranger and foreigner group behavior fictional and individual behavior real

The elements presented in this chart are cognitive and social constructs. Simply stated, they are "what we individually or collectively think." Since they involve our thoughts, facts aren't necessarily relevant. *All* the elements in the chart are subject to biased interpretations.

"How can nationality have a biased interpretation?" you may ask. Consider the following: what if you are a black Sunni Muslim of African descent that was born and raised in France having French as your primary language and fluency in Arabic. Are you French? This person will obviously fall into a number of cultural categories: black, French, Afro-French, Muslim, black Muslim, and Sunni Muslim. But which category "best" describes this person? Well, it depends. "On what?" you may ask. The short answer is the perceiver's orientation—what the perceiver believes is important (race, what they believe, how strongly they feel about what they believe, prevalent societal norms, etc.). For instance, if the perceiver was Catholic, born and raised in France and of French ancestry, they might feel threatened by what they perceive to be a non-French immigrant (nationality) or black French citizens (race) or members of the Muslim faith (religion). It's obvious that the perceiver's thoughts and beliefs (biased stories) form the basis for the way they perceive the targeted subject.

Why is this important? The stories we normalize and preserve can and often do affect our understanding of and receptivity to other cultures. It can also affect our willingness to take in and objectively evaluate the differences endemic in each group.

Cultural Shfts

Earlier I shared Dr. Jonathan Haidt's thoughts on the origins of personality. If you remember, he said that certain personality traits have "innate" origins. By innate, he wasn't talking about never changing. He was saying that the seeds of certain traits are a part of our deoxyribonucleic acidic (DNA), or as Dr. Haidt puts it, "organized in advance of experience." So we are born with a natural predisposition to certain traits that form a "first draft" of who we will become. In discussing character, we often attempt to contrast that which is "natural" (or innate) from that which is "nurtured" or organically developed. If nature refers to those traits that are "organized in advance of experience," then nurture refers to those that are "organized through experience." So we're either born with it or we develop it over time. Our one of a kind DNA makeup and the cumulative effects of our life experiences make us each wonderfully unique. Being unique causes us to see the world through unique lenses. As noted previously, we may have the same experiences but experience them differently.

Many of the stories I retain from the experiences of my youth are reflective of my unique cultural orientation. Today I self-identify as an elderly college-educated African American Christian male. The subtext of this description can be viewed as elements of culture; "elderly"—born in 1949, "college-educated"—post-graduate degree, "African"—of black descent, "American"—born in Alexandria, Louisiana, "Christian"—Baptist religious affiliation, "male"—sex. While each of these elements tells a story separately, they tell an even more refined and nuanced story collectively. I think you would agree that the story of an American male is quite different from that of an African American male born in the South in late '40s.

Every culture has its own set of stories that serve to collectively organize its members through shared experiences. Many of these stories are based on culturally significant events. For example, I am generally considered to be a "baby boomer," born somewhere between 1946 and 1964.

In addition to direct localized experiences of family, friends, and associates, there were several major national and world events that occurred that significantly affected not only me, but my entire generation, such as

- the Civil Rights and Voting Rights Acts of the mid-'60s (I was in high school and unaware of the historical and personal significance of these events at the time),
- the war in Vietnam (I had a 1-Y student deferment and a high draft lottery number, so I never had to serve),
- the Cold War with Russia (I, like many others, feared US and USSR nuclear proliferation and escalation),

- the moon landing (I don't even need to look it up—July [the month of my birth] 1969, Neil Armstrong and Buzz Aldrin, Apollo 11).

It was also a time of

- "the American Dream" (my parents were able to buy their first home, a small two-bedroom frame bungalow in a racially diverse community),
- economic prosperity (my father was able to secure gainful full-time employment, making 6K a year),
- the "Sexual Revolution" (I smoked but didn't inhale and looked but didn't touch—my story, and I'm sticking to it).

Similarly, each preceding generation had, as each subsequent generation will have, its own unique set of influencing events that will shape that group's patterns of attitudes, values, beliefs, behaviors, and stories. A perfect example is the Covid-19 pandemic; the tragic infection that has taken thousands upon thousands of human lives and will undoubtedly have a lasting impact on our social and political patterns. The formative events of my generation played a strong role in shaping how we felt about—equal rights and opportunities (Civil Rights and Voting Rights Acts), security perspective, and spending patterns (economic prosperity), antiwar sentiment (having witnessed the detrimental impact on friends and family members having participated in the Vietnam War), optimism (anything is possible), sexual freedom and high divorce rate.

These group relationships, shared experiences, and unifying beliefs serve as the bonding agent for any culture. Once ingrained, cultural changes can usually only be set into motion in one of three ways. The first is invention (create/design—scientist), the process of creating new cultural elements (impact our way of life [e.g., the telephone, the airplane, the computer, the Internet]). A second cause of cultural change is discovery (research/find—new information technology) which involves recognizing and understanding something already in existence (e.g., planets, geographic variances, other cultural traits). The third is diffusion (share with others), the spread of cultural traits from one society to another. The proliferation of new and faster technology allows us to send information around the world in seconds. Thus, the dissemination of new facts and new stories (be they true or false) is practically done in real time.

Among the most important stories we know are stories about ourselves. As previously stated, McAdams called these stories "life narratives." They are not, nor do they necessarily need to be true. McAdams describes them as simplified and selective reconstructions of the past, often connected to an idealized vision of the future"; more simply, stuff from past that influences the future. According to McAdams, these stories ultimately "influence our behavior, relationships, and mental health." In politics, conservative groups seem to give priority to policies that reflect respect for authority, group allegiance, and purity of group identity. Whereas progressives seem to prioritize policies that support equal justice, freedom of choice, and social and political diversity. These competing perspectives emanate from none other than those "life narratives."

These values and beliefs reveal themselves in the choices we make and ultimately manifest themselves in the actions we take; we sense (sensation), we think (awareness), we believe (energy), and we act (action). These values and beliefs originate not only from our parental teachings, but from numerous other environmental influences—the generation in which we were born, the culture in which we grow, the relationships in which we engage, the lifestyle in which we live. All are contributing factors to the way we think and behave.

Haven't you ever wondered…

- *Where do my* beliefs *come from?*
  - o Are beliefs the result of nature (innate) or nurture (developed)?
- *How much do I rely on* facts *when forming my beliefs?*
  - o Are the stories that I believe supported by a preponderance of evidence?

- *How do my* biases *affect the stories I create?*
  - o Am I aware of my biases and how they influence my opinions?
- *Why is it so difficult to* change *my beliefs once I have them?*
  - o Do I hold on to perspectives even when there is significant evidence to the contrary?
- *Why do I believe some people more than* others?
  - o Do I primarily believe those that I like or that agree with me or those whose opinion is supported by the evidence?
- *How do my beliefs affect my* view of the world?
  - o Are my stories generally positive and uplifting or negative and demoralizing?

Section 9: Cultural BS

- ❖ Cultural biases are biased stories (BS) about your culture and those of others
  - ➢ At any given time, there can be multiple levels of human biased systems at work; individuals, subgroups and total group.
  - ➢ The boundaries of each system can be uniquely defined to satisfy some predetermined purpose.
  - ➢ "Imposing category distinctions on groups divides the social world into different groupings" (Henri Tajfel).
  - ➢ Cultures can be distinctively defined by various combinations of elements (i.e. race, nationality, religion, etc.).
  - ➢ Individuals either self-identify or are socially organized into categorical groups.
  - ➢ The stories we normalize and preserve can affect our understanding of and receptivity to other cultures.

- ❖ Every culture has its own set of stories
  - ➢ Stories serve to collectively organize its members through shared experiences.

➤ Each generation has its own unique set of influencing events that shape the group's values and beliefs.

➤ "Life narratives" about one's culture are examples of McAdams "selective reconstructions of the past."

X. BS Reflections

Stories are life reflections. They are the culmination of individual and collective thought, a repository for reimagined experiences and the conveyors of tradition and culture. Stories implicitly reflect what we think, what we feel, what we believe, and what we value.

What Makes Our Stories Successful?

I believe the true measure of a story's success has nothing to do with structure, viability, audience connection, or contribution to society. Rather, I would argue that it's whether a story falls on the *"path of fulfilment."* In other words, "does it fulfil its intended purpose?" The stories that have lasting power are those that have the greatest meaning to you or impact on others; for instance, the memory of a significant event in your life, a statement or piece of advice that you received that was particularly impactful, *a story or joke you might have heard that was memorable, a literary piece that you authored that you are tremendously proud of.* Note that the object of each of these items—memory, event, statement, story, joke, literary piece—aren't the things that made them lasting; it's the emotion attached to them—"significant," "impactful," "proud," and "memorable." It's not the noun that uniquely defines these activities but the adjectives that we choose to describe them. Adjectives express the sentiments that energize and amplify an experience. They reflect the emotional intensity that makes the story memorable. *Since these are unique expressions of preference and are very personal to you, they are inherently biased.* Consequently, they may not have the same meaning to others as they have for you. One person's BS can be another person's "truth."

*****

Foreshadowing BS

Justice Souter once said that a Republican government wasn't threatened by foreign invasion or a military coup, but by civic ignorance. He goes on to say, "What I worry about is, when problems are not addressed and the people do not know who is responsible…some one person will come forward and say, 'Give me total power and I will solve this problem.' That is how the Roman Republic fell."

Throughout history, there have been several examples of absolute monarchs. One of the strongest absolute monarchs was Louis XIV of France. Under his rule, all legislative, judicial, and executive powers were consolidated, and he exercised final authority in all matters. Think about it. BS or not?

*****

Influence BS

We all have varying degrees of reciprocal influence on the world around us. We both *reflect and affect* the environment we live in. Our ability to influence our environment differs in both its depth and breadth—from families to communities, to regions, to nations. This is called our domain of influence. Let's assume that your domain is the local environment that you interact with daily—where you live, where you work, where you play. The stories we believe become the impetus behind the thoughts we create and the actions we take that affect that environment.

We look to our leaders to make moral and ethical decisions that can have the greatest positive impact. In all instances, the destinies of their domain of influence are determined by the stories they love and believe in. "You can't give up who you are. You can't do human activity without having human emotions" said SCOTUS Sonia Maria Sotomayor. She goes on to say "Judging is a human activity. But the sense of how you deal with it is to acknowledge it. I look at it and examine it to try to figure out the effect it's having. And then I adjust my behavior in accordance."

Disparity in values, understandings, and beliefs results in different judgments despite the same body of evidence. The information we choose to consume forms the foundation for what we choose to believe. Each person has a different response to the same stimuli (e.g., love, hate, caring, frustration, indifference). That biased perspective drives our view of the world and, more importantly, how we interact with the world. Scope of influence carries with it a greater responsibility; the greater our scope of influence, the greater our obligation to use that influence responsibly. There are many influential people who irresponsibly use their status without regard for the scope of its impact. They think that pushing their beliefs is the same as pushing the truth.

*****

Responsible BS

It would be nice if all stories evolved naturally, organically and innocently. Where we learned through rigorous study, observation and reflection versus unfounded conjecture or popular internet articles or social media. A time when we challenged concepts and theories and not people and beliefs. Where we learned to understand versus to foster self-aggrandizement. Where we strived to ensure that we were right versus to prove that others were wrong (motive). Where scientific study and qualified expertise were valued more than hyperbolic opportunism and unfounded ideologies. Where stories were created with altruistic merit versus malicious intent. If only...

Sorry, not only will it never be, it never was! Stories have always been created with a purpose, though not always conscious, and with an intent, though not always altruistic. This idealistic longing for what is perceived to be a better place and time is what I call "wishful BS." We've all had bouts of wishful BS. It's not terminal, just hopeful. But along with hopeful, they're often unrealistic. As stated previously, I would prefer "intentionally responsible BS." Intentionally responsible BS is being aware of and responsible for whatever BS you choose to consume and being honest and intentional about the BS we choose to create—aware, responsible, honest, and intentional.

These are all things that we can use to navigate the minefield of BS that we are continually bombarded with.

*****

Modern-Day Trends in BS

It is my belief (BS of course) that there have been a number of modern-day trends that have disrupted the natural process of story creation. The pervasiveness of uncompromising bias has had a detrimental impact on nuanced thinking and intellectual curiosity. These biases are being propped up by a systematic campaign of misinformation.

Politics and public service. Once honorable, moral, and altruistic, it has morphed into public relations, which has become baseless, corrupt, and self-serving (there's no bias in that story). Politicians spend all their time campaigning and creating expectations of hope and promise and, once elected, justifying their inability to fulfill those promises or, even worse, trying to convince you that they've already done what they promised. Or worse yet, they blame someone else for what they haven't done (this is often referred to as "spinning" but is often more appropriately called "lying"). When nothing gets done, the popular discord is, "I'm innocent, they're guilty," intended to absolve them of all responsibility. It has become so normalized that people expect it. A whole industry has spawned just to analyze political "spin," to discern fact from story, to separate "the chaff from the wheat." Why? Because it has become impossible for normal humanoids to do so.

Fake news. It involves using fake facts to push a false narrative that is presented as legitimate news. Fake news is actually not news at all. Fake implies neither real nor credible. News implies both real and credible. So fake news is an oxymoron. It is usually a label arbitrarily attached to a perspective someone disagrees with, even if that perspective is supported by a preponderance of relevant evidence. You can certainly use true facts to form a false narrative. These are often referred to as alternative facts, or facts selected because they support rather than prove a chosen narrative (cherry-picking—pointing at facts that seem to confirm a particular position, ignoring the larger body of evidence that exists). For example, X lied about A; therefore, X is lying about B, C, D, and E. Even if X tells the truth, 99 percent of the time or the story about A is the only lie X has told in life, X can be labeled as a "liar." That's why the word "preponderance" is so important. It implies that there is an overabundance of relevant evidence to support your perspective. Relevance means that the facts are closely related or tied to the topic at hand. "Contested numbers are everywhere, and so everyone would benefit from knowing how to interpret them," says Dr. Bell. "Statistics are often presented as the objective truth, meaning they have a particular power to make people believe a political point that is being made. But statistics are often manipulated or misused to make them appear more dramatic. So it's important to be able to spot when a statistic is being misused, so it doesn't unjustly affect our political or scientific views."

Branding. It is when a symbol, name, or phrase is recognized as uniquely representing a person or thing. As an example, consider the following:

> A person of notable fame
> whom I choose not to name
> shows no shame
> in playing the game
> of inflicting pain
> by calling others names
> tagging them with false claims
> then placing blame
> purely for political gain.

Who does this bring to mind? If you were thinking it was the former governor of Alabama and four-time failed presidential candidate George Wallace, you were right. You were perhaps thinking of someone else. No matter who you were thinking of, if you thought the description fit that person, you probably believe it's absolutely true. If you didn't, you would say it's patently false. But which is "true"? This approach is often used to brand something or someone as "good" or "bad." Proof requires facts and facts require investigative effort. It's easier to "brand" someone a "liar" than it is to prove that they're "lying." Most would rather pontificate than investigate. Pontification is the self-righteous, bombastic expression of what one believes to be factual—quite easy. Investigation is the systematic process of validating what is factual versus what is not—rather difficult. The more factual a story is, the less imagination required to create it.

*****

Rotating BS

I just recently completed reading a book which I really enjoyed. It was written in a style that I choose to call "*rotational narration*." Each chapter was written from an observer's point of view in first person. This allowed each event to be presented from multiple perspectives. Most chapters began with the pronoun "I." So if you weren't careful, you could mistakenly attribute certain thoughts and actions to the wrong character.

The reason that this style of writing is so intriguing to me is because it requires an acute understanding of human dynamics; it explores the full range of human instincts and emotions. This particular book did an excellent job of seamlessly integrating each person's history into the presentation of current events, giving deeper insights into the possible causes of their thoughts, perceptions, understanding, and responses to those events. For instance, you may see a fight break out spontaneously between two characters over a seemingly innocuous event. Interwoven into the rotating narrative is the revelation that one of the combatants just found out that the other had an affair with his wife thirty years earlier that produced a child that the first knew as the son of the wife's sister but, in reality, was his wife's son. (I just made all of that up to make a point.)

Now, put yourself in the shoes of the person who had fathered the child. What would you be thinking? What would you be feeling? Okay, now put yourself in the shoes of the husband who just found out about the child. Again, what would you be thinking, feeling? Put yourself in the shoes of the mother. Now the child. Now other spectators. Okay, I'm sure you get the picture. Each of these characters is observing the same encounter from a completely different vantage point. It's not just the event that they see, but it's the lens through which they see it.

We experience life as a "rotational narrative." We experience things—people, events, and situations—from which we form immediate impressions. Those impressions are not just the product of "what" is experienced, but the lens through which it is experienced. It's not just "what we see," but "how we see it." The "how we see it" is through the unique lens that is a natural byproduct of who we are, what we've experienced, and what we believe. Simultaneously, others are viewing the activities through their equally unique—and by the way, biased—lens.

In rotational narratives, as in life, no two perspectives are ever exactly the same. There may be many points of agreement. But the deeper you dig, the greater the possibility you will find points of departure.

Even in agreement, the reasons for agreement may differ.

I heard a politician say the other day, "We were elected by the people, so we have the obligation to do what's best for the people!"

I thought, "Ain't that the truth!"

In the next breath, he said he voted to defund a program that supported housing for the homeless. What? Do what's best for the people? What people are you referring to? Oh, I get it—the people that voted for you that aren't homeless.

There is something I call "consciousness of motive." I define it as knowingly sharing or holding on to a biased perspective to achieve some selfish motive, despite overwhelming evidence to the contrary. Therein lies the essence of *opportunistic ideologies*. The impetus for "intentional hyperbole," "fake narratives," "fictitious facts," "flagrantly biased stories," and "malicious lies" is the same—to deliberately mislead. The adjectives I used (e.g., *fake*, *fictitious*, *flagrant*, *malicious*) are to emphasize the intentionality of their distortion. This elevates the importance of being able to discern facts from interpretations and recognize the personal biases that are pervasive not only in our lives, but also in the surrounding environment. This power of discernment is needed more today than perhaps ever before. Stories are so purposefully distorted, politicized, and weaponized that it's difficult to separate fact from fiction. "Every day, Americans who shun the 'mainstream media' are taken in by doctored photos, conspiracy theories, and phony stories concocted by a mix of partisan propagandists and pranksters who enjoy stoking their outrage. Another five or ten years of this and we'll have a class of millions of citizens who get 'news' only from fake sources" ("The bogus stories that millions believe" by Michael Tomasky of *The Daily Beast*). What a sad commentary.

*****

Artistic Integrity BS

Evey Hammond, a fictional character played by Natalie Portman in the comic book series *V for Vendetta*, said, "Artist use lies to tell the truth. Politicians use lies to cover up the truth." Imagination involves forming something new—an idea, concept, or image that doesn't already knowingly exist. Before being written down on paper or committed to canvas, this new thing doesn't exist in the physical world and is merely an intangible invention of a creative mind—a fantasy. Since fantasies are, by definition untrue, they may even be legitimately called a "lie" by some. However, many of these imaginative creations can reveal or explain complex ideas in few words or a simple image—reinforcing the idiom "A picture is worth a thousand words."

There's something about artistic integrity being true to its intent—a pure, unadulterated product of someone's imagination; an artist that creates a painting with abstractions and symbols that only have meaning to them, a writer who delivers a social or political commentary that supports a cause that is near and dear to their hearts or a poet that shares their innermost thoughts and feelings by using uniquely composed aesthetic and rhythmic language—all free of any outside influences beyond the storyteller's imagination.

Monet's impressionistic paintings were less about capturing the realistic detail of a particular scene than capturing "the momentary, sensory effect of a scene—the impression objects made on the eye in a fleeting instant" (*The Art Story—Modern Art Insight: The Art Story Foundation*). Andy Warhol's symbol-filled depiction of hell was obviously not a true picture of hell. As far as I know, he didn't visit and return to share what he thought with us. I don't think it works that way. It was a pure creation of Warhol's imagination. A visual interpretation of all that he either heard, read, or otherwise believed hell to be. That's what artists do.

Einstein is purported to have said, "Imagination is more important than knowledge. For knowledge is limited to all we now know and understand, while imagination embraces the entire world, and all there ever will be to know and understand." In other words, imagination begins where knowledge ends. Imagination opens up the doors of possibility. It allows us to feel it, see it, and be it in our mind's eye before having it, knowing it or experiencing it in the real world. Through art, poetry, song, nonfiction, or spoken-word ideas take form, characters come to life and plots unwind.

*****

Noble BS

But despite the variable and paradoxical nature of BS, if after sharing a personal story, you receive the following praise from a listener: "I loved that story," or "That story was great," or "That was really enlightening," or "That was so true." It will probably elicit a warm feeling of pride, regardless of who it came from or what criteria was used to formulate that opinion. After all, who cares what others might think? At least they liked it.

But beyond the pursuit of praise, there's something about the nobility of purpose, the integrity of process, and the worthiness of outcome, all brought to life by the power of imagination that gives a story stature and longevity. All stories serve a purpose and have an impact. The most effective stories seem to be coherent narratives that have either personal, social, or cultural significance. So I've come up with a few "criteria" that I think may make a story successful. These criteria focus more on values than construction. I believe the listed criteria will help anyone create new stories with intentionality and evaluate old stories with discernment. (And of course, they're all BS.)

1. *Purpose justifies a story and answers the question "Why was this story created?"* All stories have a purpose, be they conceived consciously or subconsciously—whether it's to teach a concept, explain an idea, make sense out of a feeling, or justify an action—no matter whether it has one word or many thousand words, it still has to have a context for being. Purpose, implicitly or explicitly, gives a story focus and direction. Stories may be very private thoughts or reflections, or very public expressions of opinions, views, or impressions.

    Other questions *purpose* may answer are the following:

    *   What is the objective of this story?
    *   Why does this story exist? Why am I creating this story? "This story is to…explain / inform / instruct / influence / entertain" (inform through education, instruct through experiential learning, problem solve through visualization, explain the unknown using the known).
    *   Does / will / has this story served its purpose? (Given the explanation / information / justification you desired?)

- Was this story a conscious creation or a subconscious thought, feeling or impression, the source of which is unknown?

2. *Meaning validates a story and answers the question "Does the story effectively serve its purpose?"* Stories only endure if they are part of a larger life purpose. A story's meaning is wrapped up in the successful achievement of that purpose. Be clear on the impact of your values on the formation of your story. Decide whether your story continues to serve you well.

Other questions *meaning* might address are ...

- What is your measure of a story's success? Personal peace / joy / comfort / understanding? Public learning / support / satisfaction / wellbeing?
- Does your story serve you / others / the world well?
- Did your story have the impact intended? Did your story accomplish what you hoped it would?
- Will your story be remembered the way you want it to be long after you're gone?

3. *Integrity dignifies a story and addresses the question "Does the story fulfill its purpose with dignity?"* Integrity is the core quality of a successful and congruent story. Having integrity means being totally honest, truthful congruent in thought and deed. This implies that regardless of the story's medium, method or motive, always remaining truthful and honest in its delivery. Your purpose might be to uplift, enrich and enlighten or to discredit, defeat, and destroy. Regardless, honesty and truth should be at its core.

On the surface, discredit, defeat, and destroy may seem incompatible with truth and honesty. If we want to destroy someone, shouldn't it be by any means necessary? Not necessarily. We can discredit with facts, defeat with truth, and destroy with honor—a marriage of action and virtue. To discredit with deceit, to defeat with malice, or to destroy with hate are acts of contempt. My personal PBS is that the conscious creation of a story should be a virtuous rather than a contemptuous act, performed in honesty and truth.

Honesty and *truth* are very elusive terms. They have been and will probably always be the subject of philosophical inquiry. But in this context, I'm referring to something I choose to call "integrity of intent."

4. *Imagination animates a story and addresses the question "Does the story open up possibilities?"*

I'm a golfer (or at least I have golf clubs and I frequent golf courses). I've taken several lessons with reputable teaching pros, all to no avail. But each instructor offered me some form of visualization to help me with my golf stroke—you know, "see the ball, be ball" (from the 1980 Warner Brothers comedy *Caddyshack*). Visualization is a way to consciously engage your imagination to form mental images.

*****

"Rules of Engagement" BS

Earlier I posed a seemingly cynical question—"*Who* cares what you think?" I want to now share my answer to that same question— who cares what you think? "*I care* what you think!" And the way I hope that I show it day in and day out, despite the pervasive nature of BS in the world, is by "being objective about subjectivity." My BS is that the key to objectivity is acknowledging, understanding, and even accepting subjectivity—not just our own, but that of others. This involves being aware of and acknowledging the limitations of your own perspective, while being "curiously indifferent" or seeking to understand and empathize with the perspectives of others.

Since BS "rules", I've come up with several "rules of engagement" to help us navigate the world of BS.

1. *Respect it before you reject it.* Too often we find it difficult to "disagree without being disagreeable." In our rush to discredit someone else's BS, we personalize our disagreement, making our discourse more about the person and less about the subject at hand. We not only reject the other person's logic and rationale, but we (knowingly or not) insult their intellect and credibility. We should remember that everyone loves their BS as much as we love ours. Just as in any other committed relationship, if you attack the object of someone's affection, you can expect them to respond adversely. Instead of attacking, we should seek to understand, appreciate and empathize with the opposing perspective, even if we strongly disagree.

2. *Be fair by being aware.* Aware of self, others, and the environment. My good friends and mentors Mary Ann Rainey and Jonno Hanafin, former cochairs of the Gestalt Institute of Cleveland's International Organization and Systems Development Program, helped me understand how awareness allows people to make informed choices about whether to change or stay the same. In order to be truly aware, one must have a natural interest in the people and situations around them. Without that interest, a person may seek only to justify where they are versus exploring a different place that they could be. Remember the controversy that erupted when someone suggested that it would be more befitting to characterize Santa as a penguin than the jolly white Santa? Just think about how different that conversation might have been if both parties had a genuine interest in understanding and appreciating the perspective of the other. The principle of "awareness first" facilitates more "fairness" in the choices we make.

3. *Manage defense with curious indifference.* There's a Gestalt stance called "creative indifference," which essentially means always remaining present, aware, and open to new data. Sometimes we arbitrarily stop taking in new data when we think we have what we need. At this point, our learning often comes to an abrupt halt. Many times, once we believe something, we stop taking in information to the contrary. Believing becomes the enemy of learning. Our curiosity is squashed and judgment is limited by what we already believe. A derivative of "creative indifference" is "curious indifference." Remaining curious means not only staying open to new information, but actively seeking it. Indifference means receiving the information without pre-judging its acceptability or value. This helps us to view all data as valuable, and not just that which supports our own beliefs or of our own creation (you know, our own BS).

4. *(Don't hate, deescalate.) Don't antagonize, empathize.* The most effective way to reduce the tension in any exchange is to seek common ground. The best way to do that is to focus more on facts and less on beliefs. Facts are generally evidence or data that is observable, measurable, or historically verifiable. Beliefs are more reflective of personal opinions, feelings, and convictions. Focusing on competing beliefs is a slippery slope. It's so easy to slip into defending the "rightness" of a perspective versus its "validity" (logical or factual soundness). A well-known TV pundit gave in to this temptation when in the middle of a rather heated conversation about Santa Claus, she matter-of-factly asserted that Jesus was white. That was indeed a game changer. It not only displaced the focus of the original conversation from the competing BS about the desirable nature of Santa, but it introduced an even more controversial assertion that seemed to be an intentional effort to further escalate the already elevated tension. I would venture to guess that it probably wasn't the best move to deescalate the dialogue.

5. *Find peace in solid beliefs.* The things that elevate life's meaning are our foundational beliefs. Like Alfred Delp, I believe "when through one person a little more love and goodness and a little more light and truth comes into the world, then that person's life has meaning." Seeking doesn't have a beginning nor an end, it is truly a way of being. Solid beliefs are not the same as uncompromising beliefs. Solid beliefs are those which have withstood the rigors of challenge through the test of time. This only works if we accept challenge with openness, humility, and discernment—openness so we can hear, humility so we can appreciate and discernment so we can understand. Admittedly, some beliefs become permanent and pervasive in our lives and persist well beyond their usefulness. I believe that one way to validate and strengthen our beliefs is to continually challenge them. This allows us to consciously identify any weaknesses or flaws in our beliefs that have heretofore gone unexamined and unchallenged.

I'd like to take a moment to revisit some stories that were introduced earlier. As you read each, focus on your visceral reaction. Is there an emotional response? ("Visceral-response systems: experiential, physiological, and behavioral responses to personally meaningful stimuli; Measures of emotion: A review" by Iris and Michael D. Robinson).

Moving from abstract to concrete, do you agree or disagree with the following stories?

- Global warming is a myth. Global warming is a scientific fact.
- Capital punishment is inhumane. Capital punishment is necessary as a deterrent to capital crime.
- Gay marriage is sacrilegious. Everyone should be free to choose who they marry.
- Abortion is immoral. Abortion is acceptable in the case of rape, incest, and complications that threaten the mother's life.
- Minorities are oppressed in the US. Minorities have been key beneficiaries of US growth and prosperity.

- Any laws restricting gun ownership violate the Second Amendment rights. Common-sense gun-control measures do not violate Second Amendment rights.
- Using marijuana can result in long-term cognitive impairment. Marijuana use causes little or no long-term cognitive impairment.
- Freedom of speech is an inherent individual right. Freedom of speech should be subject to some restrictions related to respect for the rights and reputations of others.
- God created heaven and earth, and Jesus is the Son of God (Christianity). There is no God (atheism).

Which positions are BS? I would argue that they are all biased stories (BS). Some of these (particularly the last one) would cause a great deal of consternation in a lot of members of my church. Once again, if we believe something to be true, we find ways to rationalize it. And if we believe it to be untrue, we seek to find ways to mitigate or deny it.

Absolute Assertions are the enemy of nuanced thinking. An absolute assertion is a confident forceful statement of facts or beliefs that are not qualified or diminished in any way. Nuanced thinking is critical thinking or objective analysis and evaluation of an issue before forming a judgment—the rational, skeptical, unbiased analysis, or evaluation of factual evidence.

- What is your *visceral response* to the story?
- Do you have any *recognizable biases* for or against the story?
- What are the *relevant facts* of the story?
- Is *your story* supported by all relevant facts?
- Are there *other possible stories* supported by the relevant facts?
- Given all relevant facts and other possible stories, what is the *most realistic story*?

A fact is a piece of information that is "true" and can be used to support a credible conclusion. The chart that follows is an attempt to show how prevalent a role biases play in the creation of our stories.

Original BS	Biases	Fact 1	Fact 2	Concluding BS 1	Concluding BS 2
Global Warming is a myth.	The liberal scientific community is responsible for spreading this obviously untrue myth to hurt a pro-growth economic agenda.	Global warming occurs when carbon dioxide (CO2) and other air pollutants and greenhouse gases collect in the atmosphere and absorb sunlight and solar radiation from the earth's surface.	The burning of fossil fuels is the largest source of heat trapping pollutions, producing about two billion tons of CO2 per year.	We have little or no ability to affect global warming so we should get rid of regulations that negatively influence industry.	Cutting emissions and increasing the use of alternatives to fossil fuels will do little to curb climate change.
Capital punishment is inhumane.	The only reason we have capital punishment is to give the families of victims some feeling of restitution.	Capital punishment offenses include espionage, treason, select forms of murder, large-scale drug trafficking and genocide.	Death from hydrogen cyanide poisoning can be longer and more painful than other forms of capital punishment.	A more humane approach would be to allow the perpetrators of a crime to live out their lives behind bars.	Execution using hydrogen cyanide should be made unconstitutionally cruel and unusual punishment.
Minorities are oppressed in the U.S.	Minority neighborhoods have more instances of violent activity.	Racial oppression is the systematic burdening of a specific race with unjust or cruel restraints or impositions such as laws that extend to those with money and influence a level of privilege not extended to all.	African Americans are 14% of the drug users and 37% of the arrest for drug related offences, police are 80% more likely to stop blacks and Latinos, receive 10% longer sentences, 20% more likely to be sentenced to prison.	We need a greater police presence in minority neighborhoods to make them safe.	Working on a local and national scale to improve quality of legal representation, measure and monitor disparities in police activity, create collaborative community partnerships.
Using marijuana can result in long-term cognitive impairment.	Marijuana is addictive and leads to the use "harder" substances.	Active compounds of cannabis have 64 active isomers, each having different effects on human health and behaviors. Only one of these is a metabolite that can induce psychical and physical dependencies.	Cannabis has a negative impact on cognition; however, the current body of research does not provide evidence of significant, long-term effects due to cannabis use.	Use of marijuana should not be legalized and dealers should be incarcerated.	There are at least two active chemicals in marijuana that researchers think have medicinal applications. Those are cannabidiol (CBD) and tetrahydrocannabinol (THC)

Freedom of speech is an inherent individual right.	Freedom of speech is in the Constitution.	Freedom of speech is a right protected by the constitution with certain restrictions based on people's reactions to words include both instances of a complete exception and cases of diminished protection.	There are basically nine categories of unprotected speech which include obscenity, defamation, libel, slander, child pornography, perjury, plagiarism, blackmail and certain threats.	This gives me the right to say whatever I want whenever I want.	The rights of free speech are protected except in the restricted areas as recognized by the established precedent of the U.S. Supreme Court.
Santa Claus is real.	When I woke up Christmas morning, the gifts I asked Santa for ws under the tree.	Santa Claus is an imaginary figure	The legend of Santa Claus is often traced back to a monk named Saint Nicholas born around 280 AD near modern day Myra Turkey.	Don't believe my friends who say there is no Santa. Santa Claus is real.	Legends, though non-historical, are stories that often provide theoretical models for how to live positive lives as did Saint Nicholas.

Embracing BS

Many of the following quotes are familiar to many among you. Most are generally accepted as true. But let's try to reexamine each of them from a different perspective.

- *"Perception is reality!"* BS! Perception is not always based in reality. This is a notional reflection of a personal stance. Reality is a reflection of fact and truth. Perception is a reflection of values and beliefs. However, our personal perceptions are generally a derivative of our personal realities—what we believe to be true we accept as being true.

- *Sticks and stones may break my bones, but words can never hurt you!"* BS! This would only be true if we were totally void of empathy and compassion. Sticks and stones can indeed cause physical pain, but words can cause irreparable emotional distress.

- *"Justice is blind."* BS! Our perspective depends on which end of justice we're looking from. Justice is blind implies that justice is always impartial and objective. This may be true in theory, but we all know that questions of fairness, equality, and righteousness pervade our current justice system.

- *"Guns don't kill people. People kill people."* BS! It's people with guns that kill people. It's both motive (people) and means (guns, knives, hammers, spears, slingshots, skillets, etc.). Death by firearms far exceeds the sum of all others types of deaths.
- *"The end justifies the means."* BS! Machiavelli never said this, or its Italian equivalent. What he actually said is, "One must consider the final result…" (Not nearly as catchy.) Consequentialism—it implies a "morally right" act is one that produces a "good" outcome. (A good outcome for whom? You, me, us, them, all, some?)
- *"Money is the root of all evil."* BS! Here's what the Bible actually says: "The love of money is the root of all evil." Money is an "object," and love is a "feeling." The object is not the root. In today's world, money is a necessary medium of exchange. It can be used for good or evil. So money isn't in and of itself evil. It's the "feeling" about money and the "priority" that we give it that makes it evil.
- *"I disapprove of what you say, but I will defend to the death your right to say it."* BS! Voltaire—in theory, this is a beautiful thought. In practice, it says I will defend your provocations, fabrications, and violations. Really? Even the First Amendment has limitations.
- *"The only way to get rid of temptation is to yield to it."* BS! Oscar Wilde—yielding "elevates," not "eliminates" temptation.
- *"A little knowledge is a dangerous thing."* BS! This is a misquote of Alexander Pope's original statement, "A little *learning* is a dangerous thing." Learning is a process, and knowledge is an outcome. With most decisions we have a knowledge gap—from the toothpaste we buy to the politician we vote for. While a lot of knowledge is optimal, a little knowledge is certainly better than no knowledge. Learning is needed to move you along the knowledge continuum.
- *"It's the optics, stupid!"* BS! When politicians fret about the public perception of a decision more than the substance of

the decision itself, we're living in a world of optics. This quote implies that looking good is more important than being good.

- *"What doesn't kill you makes you stronger."* BS! Though well intended, what doesn't kill just may also disable, disfigure, or otherwise debilitate you.

- *"Good thoughts and actions can never produce bad results."* BS! It depends on your definition of "good" and "bad."

- *"Everyone is entitled to his own opinion, but not to his own facts."* BS! Daniel Patrick Moynihan is credited with this saying. Kind of catchy, isn't it? It sounds so good—I hate to drop this on you—but everyone can not only have their own opinion, but they can (and do) selectively choose their own facts (facts that of course support their already-held opinion).

- *"Power tends to corrupt—absolute power corrupts absolutely."* BS! This is a very eloquent statement from the British historian Lord Acton. My story is that a corrupt heart leads to a corrupt use of power; it begins inward and emanates outward. Power, like any other resource, can be used for good or evil.

The quote by Alfred Delp, the Jesuit priest who was executed for his resistance to the Nazi regime, bears repeating—"When through one person a little more love and goodness, a little more light and truth comes into the world, then that person's life has meaning" (IgnatianSpirituality.com). I believe a similar thing can be said about a story. When through a story, a little more love and goodness (*purpose*), a little more light and truth (*wisdom*) comes into the world, then that story has meaning. I choose to call this a story's "value proposition"— the thing that elevates a story to a level of worthiness—justifiably deserving of attention, admiration, devotion, and respect.

Love, goodness, light, and truth are not only high standards to meet, but even more difficult to universally define. Definitions of these terms are generally wrought with personal bias—a direct by-product of our own BS. But from my observation, the stories that seem to have lasting meaning are those that either reinforce our personal values or elicit a desired response from others. Many of us think that the stories we hold most dear are righteous, just and true, while others may see them as self-serving, condescending, and duplicitous ("righteous duplicity"—the paradox of competing BS).

I'm a believer in unbridled compassion. I think the thing that is the most divisive force in nature today is the lack of compassion. Somehow our worldly experiences have caused us to lose the boundless capacity for unconditional love that we are gifted with from birth. The innocence of curiosity, the balance of indifference, the desire for connection are all somehow muted as we venture through our worldly existence.

But no matter what we feel or what others may say, the reality still remains: *it's all BS anyway!*

*****

Section 10: BS Reflections

❖ All human dynamics involve issues of power and control.
  ➢ Power in that individuals like to be able to influence others.
  ➢ Control in that individuals don't want others to have undue influence over them.
  ➢ Influence, or the power to affect how others might think and act, is inherently biased.
  ➢ The scope of the influencer's power and control determines the extent to which human systems can be impacted.

❖ Stories don't just have power; they are the essence of power.
  ➢ Stories can influence the thoughts, actions and destinies of individuals, nations and everything in between.
  ➢ "Rotational stories" are the differing individual observations of same event.
  ➢ Values and beliefs reveal themselves in the stories that we create, choices that we make and the action that we take.

> ➢ "On our own, individuals are not well equipped to separate fact from fiction... Ignorance is our natural state (Scott Neuman, NPR).
> ➢ Cultural norms are reflected in shared stories that govern the attitudes and behaviors of all the members of that group.

❖ All stories are created for a purpose (often unknown), through a process (often unclear) for a benefit (often uncertain).
> ➢ The true measure of a story's success is whether it fulfills its intended purpose.
> ➢ Purpose doesn't necessarily have a moral compass; it can either be for "good" or "evil."

❖ Criteria that contributes to the success of any story.
> ➢ Purpose justifies a story and answers the question "Why was this story created?"
> ➢ Meaning validates a story and answers the question "Does the story effectively serve its purpose?"
> ➢ Integrity dignifies a story and addresses the question "Does the story fulfill its purpose with dignity?"
> ➢ Imagination animates a story and addresses the question "Does the story open up possibilities?"

❖ Proposed 'Rules of Engagement' to help us navigate the world of BS.
> ➢ Respect it before you reject it.
> ➢ Be fair by being aware.
> ➢ Manage defense with curious indifference.
> ➢ Don't antagonize, empathize.
> ➢ Find peace in solid beliefs.

Notes

1. Pages 8–9: *Methodist Church has reached its breaking point*, Opinion by Guthrie Graves-Fitzsimmons, a progressive Christian writer, activist and founder of The Resistance Prays. Updated 5:15 PM ET, Mon January 6, 2020.

2. Page 11: TechTerms—The Tech Terms Computer Dictionary; IPO/GIGO.

3. Pages 12–13: Marianne Bertrand of the University of Chicago and Sendhil Mullainathan of Harvard University: *Pinpointing Racial Discrimination by Government Officials*; Economic View By JUSTIN WOLFERS OCT. 6, 2017.

4. Pages 17–18: Reader's Digest: 51 Favorite Facts You've Always Believed That Are Actually False.

5. Page 23: Waldrop, M. Mitchell. *Complexity: The Emerging Science at The Edge of Order and Chaos*, pg. 33. "In life, human systems, like all other natural systems, never evolve in isolation."

6. Pages 28–29, 34, 142, 172: Haidt, Johnathan: *The Righteous Mind: Why Good People are Divided by Politics and Religion*; a 2012 social psychology book by Jonathan Haidt. 1. As Dr Haidt pointed out we are natural story processors. We are less proficient at logic processing. Rather than using logic to understand we create stories to explain our life experiences. (pg 94) intelligent people are able to generate more reasons to support any given position they decide to take.

7. Pages 29–30, 175: McAdams; The art and science of personality development. (2015) by Dan McAdams, Department of Psychology Northwestern University.
   McAdams, D. P. M. 2006, *The Redemptive Self: Stories Americans Live By*. New York: oxford University Press.

McAdams, D. P., and J. L. Pals, 2006. "A New Big Five: Fundamental Principles for an Integrative Science of Personality." American Psychologist 61:204–17.

McAdams, D. P. M. Albaugh, E Farber, J. Daniels, R. L. Logan, and B. Olson. 2008. "Family Metaphors and Moral Institutions: How Conservatives and Liberals Narrate Their Lives." *Journal of Personality and Social Psychology* 95:978–90.

8. Pages 32–33: Peter Senge's Right-Hand Column/Left-Hand Column that he presented in his book The Fifth Discipline.

9. Page 38: Jonah and the whale; Enduring Word Bible Commentary by David Guzik-Jonah 1: Jonah Runs from God.

10. Page 41: Harold Goddard. The Meaning of Shakespeare, Volume 2 by Harold C. Goddard, a professor of English at Swarthmore College. "The destiny of the world is determined…less by the battles that are lost and won than…by the stories it loves and believes in."

11. Pages 42–43: Psychology Today—Thoughts on Thinking 12 Common Biases That Affect How We Make Everyday Decisions by Christopher Dwyer, Ph.D. Some common types of cognitive biases.

12. Pages 52–56: Biblical Commentary by David Guzik from Enduring Word; 2 Samuel 12—Nathan Confronts David.

13. Page 68: Aristotle: Flat Earth, Aristotle—Spherical Earth, Modern Flat Earth Society; Evidence that the earth was spherical until about 330 BC.

14. Pages 68–69: Stanford Encyclopedia of Philosophy—Truth: First published Tue Jun 13, 2006; substantive revision Thu Aug 16, 2018.

15. Pages 69–70: The following list, which is adapted from an Auburn University whitepaper, offers some distinctions between true and false facts.

16. Pages 69–73: Auburn University: *Fact, Opinion, False Claim, or Untested Claim*—Empirical Facts, Analytical Facts, Analytic facts, Evaluative Facts.

17. Page 75: *Trump: said, "I could shoot somebody and I wouldn't lose voters"* (By CNN, Updated 12:03 PM EST, Sun January 24, 2016).

18. Page 75: Jack Nicholson—*A Few Good Men* "You can't handle the truth!"

19. Page 76: Rudy Giuliani: A former mayor of New York City famously said "Truth isn't truth."

20. Page 78: Johnny Cochran: a lawyer and civil rights activist best known for his defense of O. J. Simpson.

21. Page 78–79: Desmond Tutu guided the formation of The Truth and Reconciliation Commission (TRC) of South Africa. SAHO South African History Online—The Truth and Reconciliation Commission.

22. Page 79: John F. Kennedy, Moon Speech—Rice Stadium, September 12, 1962.

23. Page 80: FactCheck.Org: *More Donald Trump Deception on Voter Fraud*—January 26, 2017 and Los Angeles Times.

24. Page 80–82: Pew Charitable Trusts Report. An independent nonprofit research organization that provides information on worldwide social and demographic trends.

25. Pages 80–82: Brennan Center for Justice is a nonpartisan law and policy institute at New York University School of Law: Debunking the Voter Fraud Myth—January 25, 2017.

26. Page 84: New study analyzes why people are resistant to correcting misinformation, offers solutions. September 20, 2012. Researchers at the University of Michigan found that when misinformed people, particularly political partisans, were exposed to corrected facts in news stories, they rarely changed their minds.

27. Page 90: Michel Verheugh—"The months of June and July, offering 1986 the greatest and coolest UV exposure possible."

28. Page 92: ProCon.org: Opponents of medical marijuana argue that it is too dangerous to use, lacks FDA-approval, and that various legal drugs make marijuana use unnecessary.

29. Page 93: Lisa Morgan—*7 Common Biases that Skew Big Data Results*, InformationWeek—Data Management/Big Data Analytics.

30. Page 94: The Cynical Web Site is a site for cynical thinking. It contains a cynical dictionary and an index for Murphyisms.

31. Page 95: "Timing of Report by Flight's Pilot Focuses Inquiry", by Chris Buckley and Keith Bradsher, New York 2101 Times, March 16, 2014.

32. Pages 96–97: Professor Jonah Gelbach—University of Chicago Law. networks "Litigants in the American adversarial system can consult multiple witnesses on a given question but only disclose the single most favorable opinion to the fact finder (a jury, judge, or arbitrator).

33. Page 97: Tom Van Riper, a contributor to Forbes magazine, once said that Cable news try to one-up each other by rolling out programs that are hosted by people with strong, even if illogical positions on any given subject.

34. Pages 98–99: How an expert is different from a pundit by Stefan Ulstein; October 19, 2018.

35. Pages 98–99: Experts vs Pundit—What's the difference? WikiDiff.

36. Pages 98–99: The Cynical Web Site is a site for cynical thinking. It contains a cynical dictionary and an index for Murphyisms.

37. Page 101: George Orwell: Animal Farm, copyrighted 1946. Given any amount (***Squealer—opportunistic bias) In the book "Animal Farm' written by Eric Blair, better known as George Orwell,

38. Pages 102–103: Jennifer Sclafani, an associate professor at Georgetown University who studies the construction of political identity through languaged.

39. Pages 103–104: *Ted Cruz's claims about CNN are 'false'* by Brian Stelter@brianstelter February 4, 2016: 1:46 AM ET. "Ted Cruz, under fire for misinforming Iowa voters about the status of his rival Ben Carson's campaign.

40. Page 105: *Jim Inhofe Brings A Snowball to the Senate Floor to Prove Climate Change Is a "Hoax"* Kate Sheppard, Huffington Post, Feb. 2015.

41. Pages 106–107: In the article *Why People Are Irrational about Politics*" by Michael Huemer says, "The most striking feature of

the subject of politics is how prone it is to disagreement." He offers four possible theories for why political disagreements are so prevalent.

42. Pages 108–109: Rachana Pradhan *Kentucky's attempt to dismantle the Affordable Care Act.*

43. Page 109: Haidt, Jonathan, The Righteous Mind: Why good people are divided by politics and religion. Webster's Third International Dictionary defines delusion as "a false conception and persistent belief unconquerable by reason in something that has no existence in fact."

44. Page 110: William James: "A great many people will think they are thinking when they are merely rearranging their prejudices."

45. Page 112: "Proportionality" generally refers to the amount of evidence needed to prove the "truthfulness" of any given assertion.

46. Page 116: What Democrats and Republicans don't get about Robert Mueller; By Joshua Campbell; Updated 7:03 PM ET, Mon March 5, 2018.

47. Pages 122–123: Billings Gazette Trump: 'We're going to win so much, you're going to be so sick and tired of winning' by Tom Lutey, May 26, 2016.

48. Page 124: International Design Foundation; KISS principle— Keep it simple, stupid. A design principle noted by the U.S. Navy in 1960,

49. Page 125: Philanthropist Chuck Feeney—*"10 Refreshing Stories Of Rich People Who Gave Their Fortunes Away"* by Marc V. December 24, 2013).

50. Page 126–127: Bryan Stevenson—*Just Mercy: A story of Justice and Redemption.* Chapter 15 "Broken."

51. Page 129: British poet and Romanticist Lord George Byron: "But words are things, and a small drop of ink, falling like dew, upon a thought, produces that which makes thousands, perhaps millions, think."

52. Pages 129–130: Yehuda Berg: "Words are singularly the most powerful force available to humanity. We can choose to use this force constructively with words of encouragement, or destruc-

tively using words of despair. Words have energy and power with the ability to help, to heal, to hinder, to hurt, to harm, to humiliate and to humble."

53. Page 131: Gestalt approach to psychotherapy developed by Friedrich (Fritz) Perls and his wife Laura...Zinker used the "figure/ground" and "contact" concept to describe the cycle of experience. Gestalt Psychology Overview by Kendra Cherry, Psychosocial Rehabilitation Specialist and Educator; Verywell Mind.

54. Page 135–137: Sigmund Freud—Three Tiered Model of Human Consciousness; The Conscious, Subconscious, and Unconscious Mind—How Does It All Work? The Mind Unleashed: March 13, 2014 (www.mindset-habits.com).

55. Page 136: NLP (Neuro-linguistic programming) communication model we are assaulted with over 2 million bits of data every SECOND!

56. Page 144: Robert Berezin M.D.—*The Theater of the Brain.* What we attempt to create is often quite different from what currently exists.

57. Page 145: Tumblr.com—Pinterest In October 1999 an iceberg the size of London broke free from the Antarctic ice shelf.

58. Page 147: Rosabeth Moss Kanter. Harvard Business School, Author of *Rosabeth Moss Kanter on the Frontiers of Management.*

59. Page 150: Jon Ellis Meacham (born May 20, 1969) is a writer, reviewer, and presidential biographer. A former Executive Editor and Executive Vice President at Random House, he is a contributing writer to The New York Times Book Review.

60. Pages 151–152. Leo Widrich—*The Science of Storytelling: What Listening to a Story Does to Our Brains.* "If we listen to a PowerPoint presentation..."

61. Pages 154–155: auto-stereograms, Pinterest—100+ Best Auto-stereograms by Victor Canepa; where you look at a two-dimensional image that appears to be nothing more than multi-colored dots.

62. Pages 155–156: 123opticalillusions.com; Grand Illusions: grand-illusions.com—Most of us have seen the illusion that can be seen as either an older.

63. Pages 159–161: Burns, Judith, BBC News education reporter. *Fake news: Universities offer tips on how to spot it.* Adapted from the contributions of Dr Phillip Seargeant and Dr Andrew Bell. November 9, 2017.

64. Page 164: The New York Times, March 3, 2017—*Opinion | Why we Believe Obvious Untruths*, Philip Fernbach—a cognitive scientist and professor at the University of Colorado's Leed School of Business/Steven Sloman—professor of cognitive, linguistic and psychological sciences at Brown University.

65. Page 164: Scott Neuman, NPR (National Public Radio), conducted a survey that concluded "1 in 4 Americans Think the Sun Goes Around the Earth," February 14, 2014.

66. Pages 166–168: Adapted from a popular cartoon, creator unknown. Text: "For a fair selection everybody has to take the same exam: please climb that tree."

67. Page 168: W.E.B. DuBois—*The Souls of Black Folk*, a 1903 work of American literature; Commonly highlighted human differences are manmade social constructs often used to differentiate people by.

68. Page 168: Studies show that cultural differences are often the primary contributors to the gap in basic literacy and numeric skills between kids from different socioeconomic environments.

69. Page 169: Hoffman, D. H. Cognitive Psychologist—Professor Department of Cognitive Sciences at the University of California; 1986—"distorted beyond reality."

70. Page 169: According to the German Social Psychologist Henri Tajfel, "imposing category distinctions on groups divides the social world into different groupings of people" that are judged stereotypically by others (perceivers).

71. Page 170–171: Kendi, I. X.—*How to be an Antiracist*. Ibram X. Kendi, founding director of the Antiracist Research and Policy Center at American University where he is a professor of history and international relations.

72. Page 173–174: Generational Differences Chart—West Midland Family Center/Sociology Guide—A Student's Guide to Sociology (sociologyguide.com).

73. Page 179: SCOTUS David Souter on "Civic Ignorance". "What I worry about is, when problems are not addressed and the people do not know who is responsible…some one person will come forward and say, 'Give me total power and I will solve this problem.' That is how the Roman Republic fell."

74. Page 179: SCOTUS Sonia Sotomayor: "Judging is a human activity. But the sense of how you deal with it is to acknowledge it. I look at it and examine it to try to figure out the effect it's having. And then I adjust my behavior in accordance." (posted 3996 Friday, October 27, 2017, by Stephany Reyes; the Riverdale Press, May 16, 2018),

75. Page 180: Robert Driskell—"With Great Spiritual Knowledge Comes Great Responsibility."

76. Page 181: *Fake news: Universities offer tips on how to spot it* BBC News Family and Education reporter Judith Burns.

77. Page 185: Michael Tomasky of The Daily Beast "The bogus stories that millions believe".

78. Page 186: The Art Story—Modern Art Insight: The Art Story Foundation. "the momentary, sensory effect of a scene—the impression objects made on the eye in a fleeting instant."

79. Page 186: Albert Einstein is purported to have said, "Imagination is more important than knowledge. For knowledge is limited to all we now know and understand, while imagination embraces the entire world, and all there ever will be to know and understand."

80. Page 196: Consequentialism: Implies a 'morally right' act is one that produces a 'good' outcome.

81. Page 197: Alfred Delp, a Jesuit priest who was executed for his resistance to the Nazi regime, once said "When through one person a little more love and goodness, a little more light and truth comes into the world, then that person's life has meaning." (IgnatianSpirituality.com).

82. Pages 192–195: Wikipedia/ProCon.org: Pros and Cons of controversial Issues. Thebestschool.org: 25 Controversial topics to help you start your research, Apr 15, 2020, Controversial Topic Starters.

Quote References

1. Downie, J. B.: Playing the Game published by The Buzza Company, 1925—"It's not whether you win or lose, but how you play the game…"
2. Pagano, Chuck: An American professional football coach—"You're defined by how you play the game, not by the game itself."
3. Gitomer, Jeffrey: American author, lecturer and business trainer—"Great people have great values and great ethics."
4. Simpson, Don: An American film producer, screenwriter and actor—"It's not how you play the game, it's how you place the blame"
5. Earnhardt, Dale: An American professional auto racing driver—"Second place is just the first-place loser."
6. Lombardi, Vince: An American football coach and NFL executive—"Show me a good loser, and I'll show you a loser."
7. Hammond, Evey: fictional character that was the protagonist in the series V for Vendetta—A fictional character played by Natalie Portman in the comic book series V for Vendetta, said "Artist use lies to tell the truth. Politicians use lies to cover up the truth."
8. Atwater, Lee: An American political consultant and strategist—"Perception is reality."
9. Proverb "Sticks and stones may break my bones but words can never hurt you!"
10. Lustitia, the goddess of Justice in Roman mythology introduced by emperor Augusta—"Justice is blind."
11. Machiavelli—never said "The end justifies the means." What he actually said is "One must consider the final result

12. Biblical reference: 1 Timothy 6:10—"Money is the root of all evil." The Bible actually says: "The love of money is the root of all evil."

13. Voltaire "I disapprove of what you say, but I will defend to the death your right to say it."

14. Wilde, Oscar—"The only way to get rid of temptation is to yield to it."

15. The only way we can make sense out of the feedback we receive is to make connections between things, both environmental and experiential.

16. Becker, David—the director of the Center for Election Innovation and Research found:

17. Moynihan, Daniel Patrick: An American politician, sociologist and diplomat—"You can have your own opinions but not your own facts."

18. A statement supporting gun advocacy; original author unknown—"Guns don't kill people. People kill people."

19. Machiavelli: "The end justifies the means." BS! Machiavelli never said this, or its Italian equivalent. What he actually said is "One must consider the final result

20. Pope, Alexander: The most quoted 18th Century English poet other than Shakespeare—"A little knowledge is a dangerous thing." This is a misquote of Alexander Pope's original statement, "A little learning is a dangerous thing." Learning is a process and knowledge is an outcome. With most decisions we have a knowledge gap—from the toothpaste we buy to the politician we vote for. While a lot of knowledge is optimal, a little knowledge is certainly better than no knowledge. Learning is needed to move you along the knowledge continuum.

21. Acton Lord, a 19th Century British historian—"Power tends to corrupt; absolute power corrupts absolutely." BS! This is a very eloquent statement from the British historian Lord Acton. My story is that a corrupt heart leads to a corrupt use of power; it begins inward and emanates outward. Power, like any other resource, can be used for good or evil.

Book References

Dubois, W, E. B., *The Soul of Black Folk*, 1903

Haidt, J., *The Righteous Mind: why good people are divided by politics and religion*, Vintage Books, 2013.

Kendi, I.X., *How to be an antiracist*. Vintage Books, 2020.

Kouzes, J. M., B. Z. Posner, *The Leadership Challenge: How to Make Extraordinary Things Happen in Organizations*. Jossey-Bass. Fifth Edition, 1987.

Nevis, E.C., *Organizational Consulting: A Gestalt Approach*. The Gestalt Institute of Cleveland Press. Third Printing, 1987.

Orwell, G. (Eric Blair), *Animal Farm*, copyright Harcourt Inc, 1946.

Stevenson, B., *Just Mercy: A story of Justice and Redemption*. CWR, 2010.

Waldrop, M. M., *Complexity: the emerging science at the edge of order and chaos*. Simon & Schuster, 2008.

McAdams, D. P. M., *The Redemptive Self: Stories Americans Live By*. New York: oxford University Press, 2006.

Photo References

Chapter 1: Page 7
> Royalty-free stock vector ID: 525604297
>
> **Hand drawn City Sketch for your design, Drawn in black ink on white background**

Chapter 2: Page 25
> Royalty-free stock vector ID: 223037935
>
> **complexity. Joe have many things to hide. It's very complex**

Chapter 3: Page 43
> Royalty-free stock illustration ID: 1585312018
>
> **overview of the most common biases**

Chapter 4: Page 61
> Royalty-free stock vector ID: 1714496632
>
> **Vector cartoon stick figure drawing conceptual illustration of man, businessman, politician tightrope walker walking on rope with bar. Concept truth and lie.**

Chapter 5: Page 89
> Royalty-free stock illustration ID: 110687231
>
> **3d people—men, person whispered at ear.**

Chapter 6: Page 121
> Royalty-free stock vector ID: 1593215881
>
> **Vintage lettering ampersand and catchwords. Doodle catchword, hand drawn ampersands in frames and the sign vector set. Handwritten words conjurations pack. Vintage postcard, invitation design elements**

Chapter 7: Page 133
> Royalty-free stock illustration ID: 269324408
>
> **3d illustration of man holding magnifying glass looking at word text idea. 3d rendering of human people character**

Chapter 8: Page 152
> Royalty-free stock illustration ID: 276527114
>
> **3d rendering of man talking while other person with fingers in his ears pose and not listening. Concept of conflict and dispute between couple. 3d white person people man**

Chapter 9: Page 166
> Royalty-free stock vector ID: 1660914496
>
> **Group of happy friend of different religion. Islam, Judaism, Buddhism, Christianity, Hindu, Taoist. Religion diversity and Equal rights for everybody. Isolated vector illustration in cartoon style.**

Chapter 10: Page 180
> Royalty-free stock vector ID: 95708872
>
> **vector symbol of question mark in colorful background.**

Page 135—
> Royalty-free stock illustration ID: 264977984
>
> **3d illustration of thinker man sitting on a small tool with thought bubble symbol. 3d human person character and white people**

Page 158—
> Royalty-free stock illustration ID: 104723360
>
> **3d white people leaning back against a red question mark, isolated white background, 3d image**

About the Author

James Sibley is an Organizational Development Professional with a specialized certification from the Gestalt Institute in International Organization and Systems Development. He has over thirty years of leadership experience in both the for-profit and not-for-profit business sectors. He has been an independent consultant and trainer specializing in the areas of leadership and team development. James has an undergraduate degree in mathematics from Northern Illinois University and a graduate degree in finance from DePaul University (Chicago). According to James, *Who Cares What You Think?* is a product of years of contemplative thought about his own life narratives. His hope is that his personal reflections will help others see their stories as opportunities for self-discovery instead of instruments of discord.

CPSIA information can be obtained
at www.ICGtesting.com
Printed in the USA
BVHW031716160221
600262BV00001B/69